THE WORLD'S GREATEST ELECTRIC
GUITARS

THIS IS A CARLTON BOOK

First published in 2018 by Carlton Books Limited
A division of the Carlton Publishing Group
20 Mortimer Street
London W1T 3JW

ISBN: 978 1 78739 151 2

Printed in Dubai

10 9 8 7 6 5 4 3 2 1

Guitarist

PRESENTS

THE WORLD'S GREATEST ELECTRIC
GUITARS

Includes Classic, Modern, Rare and Vintage Instruments

CARLTON
BOOKS

CONTENTS

110 Gibson

INTRODUCTION

There's little doubt that the golden era of guitar arrived in the mid-20th century, with its epicentre in America during the 1950s. When you consider that Leo Fender didn't even play guitar, it's staggering how much he got right with his designs – likewise, his more traditional contemporaries at Gibson such as Ted McCarty. Our mental templates for what sounds 'good' were formed by musicians wielding the instruments these visionary designers and others made. But while instruments of this era continue to inform new designs, the hands of the luthier's clock didn't stop at the end of the 1960s. A renaissance in quality guitar design took root in the 1980s, which saw a new generation of independent makers such as PRS join the fray. The artistry of their work redefined our ideas about premium build quality and rich, nuanced tone. Meanwhile, the demands of shred guitarists such as Paul Gilbert and Steve Vai established a new branch on guitar's evolutionary tree: that of the high-performance electric guitar optimized for ultra-dextrous technical play, a style that arguably reached its apex in Vai's famous JEM series of Ibanez electrics, which continues to evolve. Today, we can see these two strands of guitar design converge in high-end electrics. With this dazzling vista of guitar greatness before us, we've set out to present some of the finest and rarest existing examples of milestone instruments in this compendium of tone, along with some bleeding-edge examples of great guitar design in the present day. We hope you enjoy this evocative journey into the art of the guitar as much as we enjoyed making it.

Jamie Dickson,
Editor–in–Chief, Guitarist

BC RICH

MOCKINGBIRD

They may have achieved their notoriety in the hands of rock's more sinister practitioners in metal guitar's 1980s heyday, but the pointy and powerful BC Rich range was the brainchild of a flamenco player and luthier who began his career creating acoustic guitars in LA in the 1950s. Bernardo Chavez Rico's first original designs were through-neck creations, which evolved throughout the 1970s and 80s into the outrageous metal weapons wielded by the likes of Joe Perry, Tony Iommi, Blackie Lawless, then later, Slash and Josh Homme to name but a few.

The Mockingbird debuted around 1976, and along with 1978's Bich and 1980's Warlock, left a fluorescent imprint on guitarists' minds. The Mockingbird was a through-neck, twin-humbucker, mahogany-bodied affair with a loud, sustaining call, and a pronounced lower bout creating a beaky profile. Its various incarnations have incorporated Floyd Rose vibratos and flexible switching systems according to prevalent musical trends. The Mockingbird is still available today, in an array of options.

BRIAN MAY

RED SPECIAL

The Queen guitarist has one of the most recognizable and sought-after tones in rock – and it still beggars belief that part of that great sound comes from a guitar he made with his father in the family's garden shed 50 years ago.

Over the years many have striven to unearth the Red Special's secrets by building their own versions, but none have really come close. May brought out affordable copies under his own name in 2004.

Former *Guitarist* magazine stalwart Simon Bradley not only co-wrote the definitive book on Brian May's Red Special; during the process he actually helped take it apart, too, for a forensic examination of this unique, priceless and irreplaceable instrument. So no pressure, then.

"I was lucky enough to get my hands on the Red Special for the first time in 1999 and was immediately struck by the neck; its girth was more substantial than any other electric I'd played and the action was almost impossibly low," Simon explains. "Upon closer inspection, the guitar was in surprisingly good nick, especially considering the sheer amount of use it'd had over its life thus far. Yes, there were plenty of nicks and marks on the body, but the fact that it worked so effectively – and that it still does – is testament to its hardy construction."

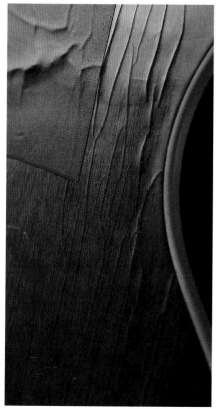

BURNS
MARVIN

Burns guitars flew the flag for British guitar design in the 1960s. The twin-horned, originally four-pickup-sporting Bison may be the Alpha design, but it's the Marvin that remains most fêted by Burns aficionados. Designed in conjunction with its eponymous endorsee, the Marvin went through a 24-month gestation and around 30 prototypes before it became Hank's main squeeze between 1964 and 1970, at which point, as he puts it: "My guitars were stolen, never to be seen again, well not by me!"

Designed with the Stratocaster as its jumping-off point, the Marvin had a similar scale-length and circuitry. It differed in its distinctive scroll headstock and mahogany body, however, and featured the newly designed Rezo-Tube 'Tremolo' with a knife-edge pivot and individual tubes for each string, and distinctive Rez-o-Matik single-coil pickups. Around 300 Marvins were made in the company's original incarnation, with more recent reissues made by Burns London including this 50th Anniversary Dream.

COREY CHRISTIANSEN MODEL ARCHTOP

A modern masterpiece of an archtop that marries progressive thinking with time-honoured luthiery.

This breathtaking modern creation was born from the collaboration of two talents at the very top of their game. It was crafted by North Carolina-based luthier John Buscarino for US jazz picker, Corey Christiansen, and combines a number of intelligent modern tweaks to the classic archtop formula.

As you'd expect from a man who learned from classical guitar master-builder Augustino LoPrinzi and archtop maker Robert Benedetto, it's an exquisite instrument, featuring a solid carved aged Sitka spruce top married to Big Leaf flamed maple back and sides. It also incorporates a feedback-suppressing block inside the body, and has an Alnico III pickup wound by Kent Armstrong.

CARVIN

ALLAN HOLDSWORTH HH2

Today, the long-established Carvin brand is a diverse entity, and its most high-profile product is the Steve Vai-endorsed Legacy amp. Yet its Custom Shop creates guitars, too, and one such custom-order specimen is the 2012 Carvin Allan Holdsworth HH2, created to the preferences of the jazz virtuoso.

A throwback to the pioneering anachronism that was the Steinberger guitar of the 1980s, the HH2 is also headless; however, despite still being diminutive and lightweight, it has a larger body than its predecessor, and is constructed from chambered Alder rather than hi-tech plastic. It's a sonically versatile guitar, and produces full tones characterized by blooming feedback tails that belie its stature, particularly with plenty of gain. As you'd expect, there are jazz tones nestling in the bridge and neck humbuckers, and 24 frets and a 25.5-inch scale offers plenty of options for more adventurous fretboard excursions.

COLLINGS

I35LC

How fastidious is Bill Collings when it comes to building guitars? Well, during the R&D process for the I35LC model – based of course on Gibson's genre-defining ES-335 – he realized he didn't much like the quality of the commercially available plywoods for the guitar's construction… so he acquired a massive pressing machine to make his own maple laminates!

Unlike the 16-inch wide Gibson ES-335, the I35 has a smaller 15-inch body, which makes it easier to handle for many players and perhaps more tonally balanced, too. The set neck is mahogany, with a long-tenon design for rigidity, mass and sustain.

The I35LC resembles the ES-335 in terms of its electronics and hardware complement, using vintage-inspired humbuckers made by Jason Lollar that have a slightly higher output than those on the solid-wood I35 model. The tonal results are a wonderful blend of fatness, good articulation and impressive versatility for myriad musical styles.

Collings is a premium guitar maker, so the cost of entry to the I35 club is suitably high, built by a discerning maker, for an equally discerning customer.

DAN ARMSTRONG

PLEXI

During The Rolling Stones' 1969 US tour, Keith Richards was spotted with an unusual double-cut apparition. It featured a body made of polymethyl methacrylate, a tough acrylic thermoplastic marketed under brand names such as Lucite, Plexiglas and Perspex. The guitar was dubbed the 'see-through', but became better known as the 'Plexi'.

Designer Dan Armstrong was hired in 1968 by US manufacturer Ampeg to give its existing range a makeover. His innovations didn't stop with the plastic. The maple neck had a revolutionary 24-fret rosewood fingerboard, while Formica sheets made up the faux wood scratchplate. The single Bill Lawrence humbucker could be installed and removed in seconds, and Ampeg offered six pickup models of varying output to allow owners to customize the guitar's tone as fast as they could swap them over.

DANELECTRO
U2

A triumph of engineering ingenuity and creative cost-cutting, Danelectro guitars are an icon and a success story of the post-war US society of the 50s and 60s, right down to their rudimentary build and 'can-do' attitude. Created by Nathan Daniel and initially distributed by the Sears-Roebuck mail order company bearing the Silvertone brand name, these beginners' instruments were quirky, affordable, and extremely popular. Their distinctive twangy, cutting tone (created in part by their unique hollow-body Masonite construction and lipstick tube pickups) may have been borne from necessity, but it nonetheless found its way into the gear arsenals of legendary guitarists, including Jimi Hendrix, Jimmy Page and Eric Clapton among many others.

The U2 model was originally made between 1956 and 1958, and was reissued a number of times from the 90s onwards. Its single cutaway body shape comprises a poplar frame and Masonite top and back with vinyl binding, and its twin pickups were wired in series rather than the more traditional parallel configuration.

DELICE

FUTURAMA III

Made in former Czechoslovakia and imported into the UK by Selmer, the Futurama was the guitar to aspire to for practically every young hopeful in British beat groups of the late 50s and very early 60s. The prohibitive price of imported Fenders and Gibsons at the time meant that the Futurama's comparatively modest price tag was just about reachable for the more serious player. This was certainly the case for George Harrison – who took a Futurama to Frankfurt with The Beatles – and fellow Liverpudlian Gerry Marsden from Gerry And The Pacemakers. Even Jimmy Page had a Futurama at one point during the dawn of his career.

Early Futuramas were built in Blatna at the Drevokov Cooperative in Czechoslovakia and featured a faux-maple fingerboard and a surface-mounted jack socket. Later models – such as the one featured here – were manufactured in Hradec Králové by CSHN, the major hardware change being the jack socket, which was now edge-mounted.

When Fender switched to rosewood 'boards at the close of the 50s, Futurama followed suit, dyeing a cheaper hardwood (quite possibly beech) accordingly. "They followed Fender and went for a darker wood," Phil Carwardine of Vintage And Modern Guitars tells us. "But it's a cool thing in that a Fender Strat was something to dream about in '58/'59 in the UK, so loads of people had these and, actually, when you look at them, they're not that bad – there's quite a bit in them. It's quite engineered, really. You can get Hank out of it, which is what everyone was doing, I guess, wasn't it?"

DUESENBERG

POMONA 6

This inspiring halfway house between lap and pedal steel incorporates an ingenious Multibender bridge, with two levers to add pedal-steel bends to your slide excursions.

A Hawaiian-style instrument, it also has a movable capo for key changes and a pair of roaring Little Toaster pickups. A great idea, well executed. Slide away!

EPIPHONE

CASINO

Introduced in 1961, Epiphone's version of new parent company Gibson's ES-330 marked a departure from the often luxurious large-bodied archtops that had established the company's name. A fully hollow design with limited upper-fret access, twin P-90s and more primitive appointments than Gibson's semi-hollow ES-335, it was its imperfection that led to the Casino's ace in the hole – its association with The Beatles. Paul McCartney bought his because he wanted a guitar with hollowbody tone: Lennon and Harrison followed suit, and the Epiphone Casino was duly immortalized.

EPIPHONE

ZEPHYR DE LUXE REGENT

A heavenly hollowbody from the jazz era with luxury appointments and twin humbuckers, Gibson didn't have the monopoly on cool hollowbody electrics in the 50s, as this royally appointed Epiphone attests. Despite its 1957 pedigree, the jazz-era stylings, such as the elegant 'Frequensator' tailpiece, hark back to the earliest versions of the model, which was introduced in 1948. In fact, the De Luxe Regent – sold as the Deluxe Electric in its latter years – was discontinued the year after this model, equipped with two New York mini-humbuckers, was made. During the model's lifespan, the body width grew from 17.75 to 18.5 inches in some mid-50s examples. This particular Zephyr, shot while residing at Vintage 'n' Rare Guitars, Bath, sports a blonde finish on its laminated spruce top, but the model was also available in a Sunburst. What's it like to play? Well, of course, it's a breeze…

ERNIE BALL MUSIC MAN

AXIS SUPER SPORT

Music Man has a well-earned reputation as the producer of some of the most comfortable and tonesome guitars around and the Axis, loosely based on the lauded EVH Signature from 1990, is one of the most popular.

With a distinctive 4+2 headstock configuration, bijou body design and a wonderfully playable birds-eye maple neck that's lightly oil-finished, the range includes models loaded with a Piezo pickup system, a double-locking Floyd Rose vibrato and a recent number from the sumptuous Ball Family Reserve line.

In fact, the singlecut template was used for more outlandish innovations such as the Game Changer, but the feel and light yet forceful tones are constant across the board.

There aren't many guitar companies that can boast such diverse endorsers as John Petrucci, Steve Lukather and Albert Lee, but a single strum of any US Music Man guitar will immediately explain why.

ESP
GL-56

George Lynch is a formidable technician who earned plenty of respect with his flurries of trademark Phrygian scales, and his numerous signature guitars have remained a cornerstone of ESP Guitars' signature roster since 1986.

The eye-popping Kamikaze was the first, but this distressed S-type is based on a guitar the ESP Custom Shop built for him prior to the former's introduction. The wear is beautifully done and applied by hand, using sandpaper and various tools as well as – according to ESP head-honcho Matt Masciandaro – fire and water…

Electronics include a Seymour Duncan Pearly Gates humbucker, an unashamedly PAF-style of pickup that's in stark contrast to the high output tone of Lynch's signature Screamin' Demon model, and the gorgeous neck bristles with 22 of the biggest frets you're ever likely to encounter. It's now discontinued from the Japanese ESP range, but there are other 'aged' ESPs to tempt you.

EVH

FRANKENSTEIN REPLICA

Back in 2007, Fender's Custom Shop launched a 300-only run of one of its most ambitious creations ever – a breathtakingly faithful replica of Eddie Van Halen's beloved bitsa, nicknamed 'Frankenstein'. The pricetag of $32,000USD (circa £16,000) was, admittedly, a stumbling block for some players, to say the least. But when we got our trembling paws on one to inspect, we played it, caressed it and just sat staring at it in awe, wondering how it was possible to recreate something so unique, so faithfully.

Of course, the original – like Frankenstein's monster, the product of hours of frenzied experimentation with guitar parts lying around Wayne Charvel's San Dimas repair shop – wasn't put together with anything like as much care.

"You know, I bought a body from them for 50 bucks and a neck for 80 bucks, slapped it together, put an old Gibson pickup in it, and it's my main guitar," shrugged Ed at the time. "Painted it up, you know, with stripes and stuff. I guess that's my thing."

But for Fender's Custom Shop team, reproducing it to the last fibre became an obsessively vintage-correct labour of love. From finding the correct materials to matching the finish to painstakingly sourcing the precise make of cycle reflector that Eddie absent-mindedly stuck to the guitar's back, the Frankenstein Replica is – for all intents and purposes – an identical guitar to the one it's based on.

Considering the rich history of the original, the significance of both Van Halen's music and Ed's stunning technique, plus the frankly amazing level of detail that had clearly gone into the manufacture of each example, we concluded (as we reluctantly handed it back) that the guitar blurred the line between a practical instrument as we know it and a work of art.

EVH

WOLFGANG USA CUSTOM

Edward Van Halen's appearances may have been sporadic of late, but the guitars he uses still attract massive attention. Having cut the umbilical cord from his iconic, Stratocaster-style Frankenstein, Ed opted for an all-new design, first with Ernie Ball Music Man and then Peavey. Now he has his own brand: EVH. Named after his son and bandmate, the Wolfgang is a wonderfully made, modern rock guitar. Models include the Special and this rather gorgeous Custom. Unusually for a Van Halen-inspired guitar, the Custom has a traditional fixed bridge on a maple-capped mahogany body, though Ed's personal guitars always feature a vibrato. This model also has an ebony fingerboard (instead of the usual maple), a feature that Ed has come to enjoy in recent years, All up, the Custom is designed to appeal to players that sit more on the Gibson (rather than Fender) side of the guitar fence.

FANO

ALT DE FACTO JM6

An intriguing blend of Fender playability and aesthetics and Gibson-like switching, and with a sound tantalisingly poised between the two extremes, the Lindy Fralin P-90-loaded JM6 is a (reasonably well-heeled) alt-rocker's dream companion. Simultaneously reassuringly familiar and yet still somehow unique, vintage-vibed retro doesn't come much more individual than this.

ALT DE FACTO RB6 THINLINE

If, at first glance, the RB6 reminds you of about three or four classic guitars all at once, that's because it's inspired by maker Dennis Fano's vision of "an alternate reality where the great American luthiers of the 1950s work together under one roof". Once you're over the sumptuous retro craftsmanship and tactile 'medium distress' relicing, plugging the RB6 in delivers a similarly shapeshifting experience. The combination of a TV Jones Power'Tron in the neck and a Lollar 1952 Tele bridge pickup seated in a Telecaster-style bridgeplate assembly provides familiar Fender-esque twang, accentuated by the Thinline body but offset in equal measure by a 628mm (24.75-inch) scale length and chunky neck that's altogether more Gibson-like in feel. The RB6 is a unique and beautiful creation, and the ultimate proof that a Frankenstein guitar can provide a monster playing experience.

FENDER

Nocasters, Broadcasters, early Stratocasters, Jags and Jazzmasters... Fender's legendary guitar models are responsible for the large majority of vintage-guitar folklore, and some of the very rarest and most desirable we've come across are lined up here for your delectation.

FENDER

BROADCASTER

The first-ever mass-market solidbody was a masterstroke of pragmatic engineering. Leo Fender's Broadcaster was the first mass-produced solidbody electric guitar; an ingenious instrument designed with an engineer's love of practicality firmly in mind. From its twin pickups with contrasting tone and bolt-on neck with newly installed truss rod, to its feedback-eliminating alder body, every decision made on the drawing board was to prove an enduring and unqualified success. In fact, the only mis-step was the name: as is well-documented, Gretsch had already copyrighted its Broadkaster drum kit, and the Telecaster was born. This example, from the first year of its release, belongs to Guitars: The Museum.

FENDER

CABRONITA

The Cabronita's success may well have taken Fender by surprise. While it looks like a genuine 1950s design, the first of its kind was in fact the Fender Custom Shop El Cabronita Especial that debuted in 2009, in both single- and twin-pickup variants. Using Gretsch-style humbucking pickups in a Telecaster chassis, the general idea is all about simplistic, stripped-down, old-school cool. Since those early Custom Shop models, a slew of vintage- and modern-leaning Cabronitas have been released under the Fender and Squier marques, adding Bigsby vibrato units, Fideli'Tron and Power'Tron pickup options, and a lightweight Thinline version for good measure. Regardless of the flavour you opt for though, it's clear from the moment you plug in that the Cabronita revels in its badboy image, can't wait to hit the stage, and deserves its burgeoning status as a modern classic.

Pictured right, Fender's entry-level 'Especial' Squier version of the Cabronita flanked by Fender Custom Shop Luchador (Strat-style) and Boracha (reverse Jazzmaster-style) variants.

FENDER
ESQUIRE

Looks like a Telecaster, right? Well, Fender's single-pickup Esquire actually predates its more famous brother. The earliest appeared in 1950, commonly with black-finished pine bodies. The Esquire was, for all intents and purposes, the blueprint for every electric solidbody guitar that followed. Soon after, Fender made two-pickup Esquire prototypes, moving to an ash body instead of pine. That variant was subsequently renamed 'Broadcaster', the guitar that by 1952 would forever more be known as the Fender Telecaster. Despite having only one pickup, Esquires still had a three-way selector switch that offered access to three sound variations. Position one is often the bridge pickup, straight to the output. Position two brings the volume and tone controls into play, while position three introduces a tone circuit for a more muffled/bassy sound. Esquires are often jokingly referred to as 'a Telecaster without the other pickup that you don't need', something with which Bruce Springsteen and ZZ Top's Billy Gibbons would surely concur.

FENDER
1962 JAGUAR

Fender's feature-packed surf oddity has endured to become a go-to choice for indie guitarists. January 1962 saw Fender assemble its first Jaguars, and by March of the same year the model began to roll off the production line in significant numbers. At $379.50 in Sunburst, it was $90 pricier than the Strat, and in keeping with its top-end status, the Jag bristled with features. The combination of a spring-loaded string mute, lead and rhythm circuits, a low-end filter nicknamed the 'strangle switch' and a 24-inch scale length made it a little fussy for many. Despite the high-profile endorsement of Beach Boy Carl Wilson, sales quickly waned, though the patronage of legions of indie rockers in recent decades has served to rehabilitate the Jag's reputation.

Pictured is a unique green sparkle '62 Jaguar that was painted in an auto shop near Fender's factory in Fullerton as a custom finish. It's currently on display at the Songbirds Guitar Museum in Chattanooga USA.

FENDER

1962 FIESTA RED JAGUAR

Similar in shape and general design to its stablemate, the Jazzmaster (which Fender introduced in 1958), the Jaguar made its debut in 1962. This particular specimen from the first year of production is finished in Fiesta Red, which would have been a custom colour option as the stock Jag was originally offered in Sunburst as standard. It also began life at the time when Fender was changing over from 'slab' rosewood 'boards in favour of the marginally less collectable veneer variety. Phil Carwardine from Vintage And Modern Guitars in Thame agrees: "Sadly, it's just a veneer 'board, it's not the slab 'board," he says, referring to the model before us. "They didn't make many of those. It came in just at that time." Of the other attributes the Jag has to offer, Phil continues: "It's got a 24-inch [609.6mm] scale length, which I like – that's just about the most predominant feature of the Jag, isn't it? And the switching system, which you either love or hate. Get the right strings on it and they're great!" The other Marmite feature of the Jaguar was its vibrato, ostensibly a more sophisticated system than the Strat, featuring adjustable spring tension and the ability to lock the entire mechanism if you want to go *au naturel*. This particular model has a painted headstock, something we see more of these days, but was considered quite unusual at the time. "It was the Jazz and the Jaguar that got the matching headstock," says Phil. "I think they started doing it around 1962. It was a surf thing. The Coronados got it, didn't they?" The Jaguar enjoyed a resurgence in interest when new wave bands took it up in the late 70s – notably Tom Verlaine from Television, also a proponent of the Jazzmaster – and then again in the 1990s in the hands of players such as Kurt Cobain.

FENDER

JOHNNY MARR JAGUAR

In 2012, a collaboration between Fender, Johnny Marr and a team of UK design cohorts on Marr's signature Jaguar resulted in a series of player's-eye-view refinements – some technical, some aesthetic. Among them were a neck shape based on Marr's beloved 1965 model, a new bridge design and refinements to the electrics and vibrato; and the unanimous verdict was that Johnny's Jag was the best-sounding example of the model yet.

FENDER

JAZZMASTER

Maligned and misunderstood it may be, but with the benefit of hindsight, Fender's Jazzmaster was definitely misnamed. Introduced in 1958 as a solidbody rival to the archtops that dominated jazz, it was roundly ignored by the players in the genre, and had to settle instead for a lifetime of being appropriated by sonic youths. The first generation to bend Leo's offset misfit to their needs was the surf crowd, who put its temperamental yet mechanically advanced vibrato system to great use until Fender introduced the surf-specific Jaguar in 1962. Despite being Fender's flagship model, by the mid-1970s, the Jazzmaster found itself unwanted and unloved. Seemingly doomed to languish in secondhand stores for the rest of eternity, it was rescued for a second time. The likes of Elvis Costello and Television's Tom Verlaine played them in their late-70s heyday, and they were followed by a wave of alt-rockers such as Sonic Youth and J Mascis of Dinosaur Jr, who redefined the Jazzmaster as an outsider's noise-making machine.

THURSTON MOORE'S 1958 JAZZMASTER

Thurston Moore's experimental guitar exploits with Sonic Youth and in his solo career have influenced countless guitarists to mod their instruments, exploit different tunings and try to channel the howl of feedback for musical ends. "I've never really been a guitar geek!" he told us. "I realize that I've been sort of a poster boy for guitar geekdom to some degree… but I've never been a guitar geek myself." Two guitar models in particular owe Thurston and his Sonic Youth guitar partner, Lee Ranaldo, a huge debt. For most of their career, the band used (and fearlessly modded) Fender Jazzmaster and Jaguars among other models, and this example is Moore's recent touring and recording squeeze. "That's a first series '58 Jazzmaster," he says of the battered but defiant guitar, which you can hear on Thurston's 2014 solo album, *The Best Day*. "It has a Mastery bridge and the Mastery vibrato unit. It's surprising how much you can use those [units] and not see your tuning go all over the place."

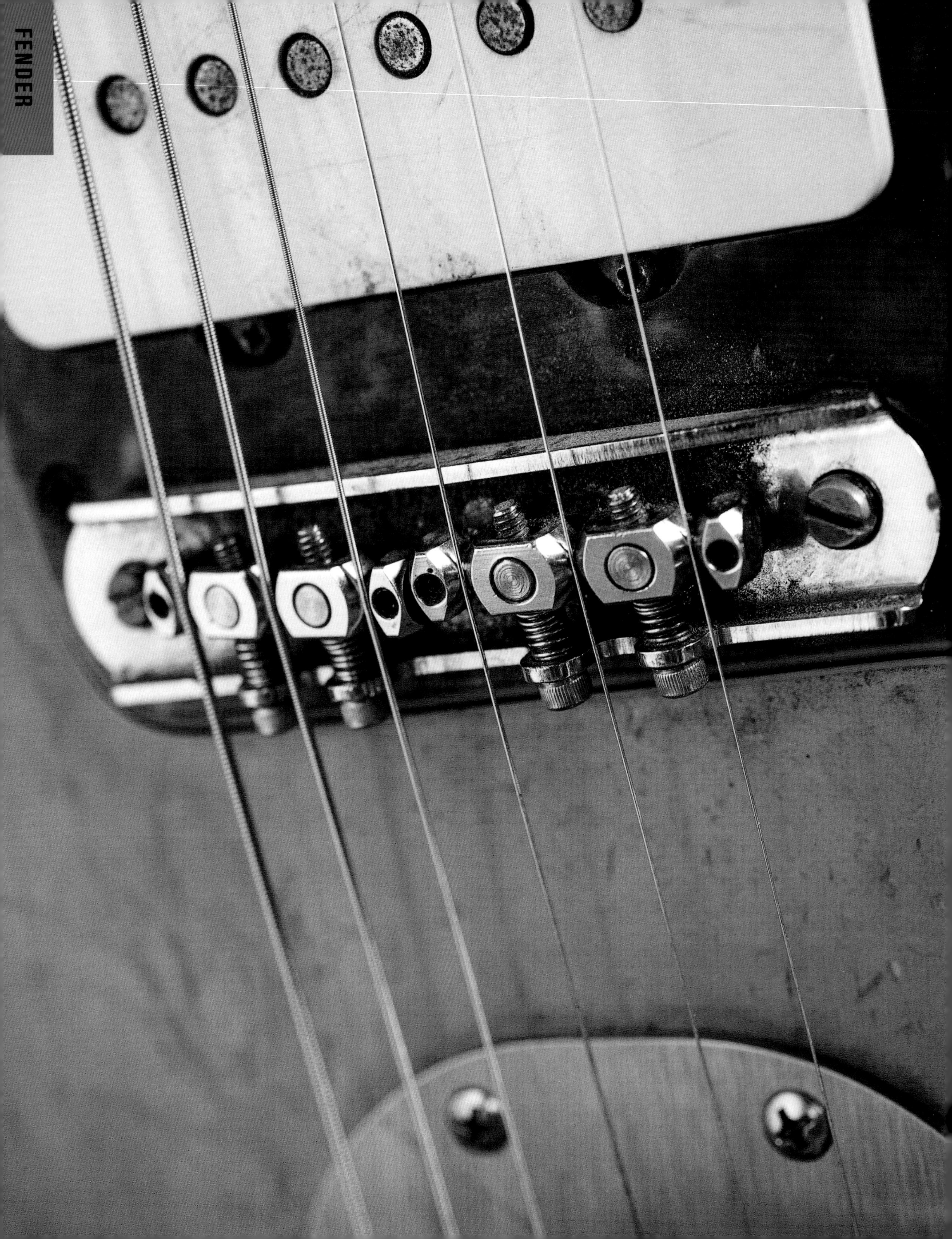

FENDER

MODERN PLAYER STARCASTER

Fender released the Starcaster in 1976 as an attempt to break into the market-share enjoyed by Gibson's semi-hollowbodied ES-335 family. After underwhelming sales, it was discontinued in 1982 and crated up to join the Lost Ark, untouched and unloved by the general public. However, a small but dedicated indie following, and the patronage of Radiohead's Jonny Greenwood, eventually led to enough demand for Fender to update and resurrect it in 2014, albeit in much-modernized form. The original's Seth Lover-designed Wide Range humbuckers are reproduced, though, and it's their tone, coupled with the instant familiarity afforded by that bolt-on neck design, that will inspire a new generation of effects-loving indie kids to fall for the Starcaster's offset quirkiness all over again.

FENDER
MUSTANG
(KURT COBAIN ARTIST EDITION)

Fender's Mustang wasn't the company's first entry-level guitar, but its timely arrival in 1964, when guitar music was hitting an all-time peak, ensured it would be a success. Incorporating a Dynamic Fender Vibrato system which fixed to the top of the body, and tipping its hat to the Jazzmaster with its similar bridge and offset waist, the model came in either 22.5- or 24-inch scale-lengths. It had two pickups akin to those of the Duo Sonic model, its very similar predecessor, but with two slider switches to select 'lead', 'rhythm' or 'off' settings. Available in either red, white or blue, the Mustang was simplicity itself. The 1990s saw interest in the Mustang rekindled, mostly due to Nirvana's Kurt Cobain, who immortalized the model by wearing it in the video to 'Smells Like Teen Spirit'. Fender waited until 2012 to release a tonally versatile signature model, which resembled the Nirvana frontman's 1969 Lake Placid Blue model with its Competition Stripes, but added a humbucker in the bridge position.

FENDER

NOCASTER

Fender's famous guitar with no name has become a Holy Grail for vintage collectors. Players of a certain mindset might assert that if you can't do it with the combination of an early 1950s Telecaster and a '58 Bassman then you are doing it wrong. Staunch purism aside, even the modernists among you will likely find your hearts all aflutter at the sight of this pair of sassy blondes. The instrument on the left is one of two 'Nocasters' at Guitars: The Museum, in Umeå, while the 1954 Telecaster on the right showcases all of the features that were phased in during the second half of that year: a White Blonde finish, a single-ply vinyl scratchplate and the steel saddles that further brightened the Tele's already twangsome tone. That 'butterfly' string tree is presumably a later addition, as they didn't arrive until mid-'56. The '51, meanwhile, has a round string tree and slot head screws, as an original Nocaster should. It looks as if it's been played a whole lot more, too…

STRATOCASTER

❖

FENDER
1954
STRATOCASTER

Here's where it all started – a first-year example of the world's most enduringly popular electric guitar. Ask any kid with a crayon to sketch a guitar, and this is what they'll draw: the Fender Stratocaster, the best-selling and most famous design of them all. This original 1954 specimen, from the year of the Strat's debut, currently resides at Umeå's Guitars: The Museum, and if you could see it with fresh eyes, imagine what a mind-blowing spectacle it would've been for the musicians of the era. The body contouring, versatile and musical Synchronized Tremolo, the adjustable saddles on the sprung, string-through-body bridge assembly and the offset third pickup were perfectly in tune with both the demands of the working musician – thanks to the input of Western Swing guitarist Bill Carson – and the horizons of the space age that inspired its name. Little wonder, then, that Fender's masterpiece went on to dominate popular music, and remains, pound-for-pound, the most versatile electric guitar design, a whole six decades later.

FENDER

1956 HARDTAIL STRATOCASTER

When Fender's Stratocaster was first released in the spring of 1954, one of the outstanding features of its futuristic design was its vibrato unit. Today, of course, everyone knows about the 'spring tension vs string tension' balancing act that went on to make some of rock 'n' roll's classic guitar moments and many have tried to overhaul and improve on Leo's initial design. But for many, only the original will do and it's a system that has become synonymous with both the look and sound of the instrument for decades. So, perhaps it was a surprise when, in March 1955, the first non-vibrato models began to appear on the market, Fender perhaps wisely figuring that, for some players at least, the twang wasn't necessarily the thang after all. We don't have the exact figures for how many hardtail models were made at the time, but, even today, they are comparatively rare. When you add in the appeal of a vintage model such as the 1956 Sunburst example we have here, you're talking about a very rare breed.

The non-vibrato Strat has quite a devout following, its disciples maintaining that a perceived difference in tone (more focus, less shimmer) and the lack of fuss when tuning – anyone who has restrung a Strat with a vibrato will know only too well how cantankerous the device can be – only enhances what is, for them, the perfect electric guitar.

The example we have here is remarkably clean – just look at the lack of wear to the fingerboard, and the body looks like it has been in careful hands all its life, too. It all adds up to being a very rare beast indeed and, who knows, it might just convert someone to the subtle charms of hardtail Strat ownership.

FENDER

RORY GALLAGHER'S 1961 STRATOCASTER

Up close and personal with the 1961 Stratocaster played almost to destruction by the late, great Rory Gallagher. Rory's famous '61 Strat, the one he played so hard that only a few jagged islands of lacquer remain on its body, while its reverse still bears a faint blue sheen from his jeans, is truly one of rock's iconic instruments. Reputedly the first in Ireland, it was originally ordered by a player in another showband; but he wanted a Hank-alike red to complement new stage outfits, not the sunburst that arrived. When the red one appeared, this went back to the shops: Rory bought it, on credit, a few months later. Heavily modified due to the duress of a thousand boiling-hot gigs, nowadays, the Strat's neck and body are among the instrument's few remaining original parts: the scratchplate, tuners, two of the pickups and the five-way pickup selector are all non-stock. Perhaps the biggest change it underwent, though, is the most obvious – the original three-tone Sunburst finish, dissolved by its owner's sweat over the years, is a testament to the love this uniquely skilled and much-lamented workman had for this simple tool.

FENDER

1963
STRATOCASTER

For many players, the Strat reached its apex in the early 60s. The reputation of guitars from this era among players was such that when Fender's fortunes were waning in the early 80s, after buyers had become disillusioned with CBS-era Strats, a slab-'board 1962 model was selected as the basis for a new series of historically accurate reissues that helped turn the company's fortunes around. By 1963, however, the Strat had moved on again. To address production problems Leo Fender had experienced with slab-fretboard necks, he introduced round-laminate 'boards part-way through 1962, which entailed gluing a thin, curved layer of rosewood onto the top surface of a maple neck that had already been cut to the correct radius. It was a trickier piece of workmanship to complete and marked a new phase in the guitar's development.

This battered but beautiful '63 Stratocaster in Fiesta Red is currently on show at Guitars: The Museum, a permanent exhibition in Umeå, Sweden. It's a long journey north, unless you currently reside at the Pole, but if you want to feast your eyes on this gorgeous slice of Strat history, you could do a lot worse than pay a visit.

FENDER

PHILIP SAYCE'S 1963 STRATOCASTER

Welsh-Canadian blues-rocker Philip Sayce is the proud owner of what's left of this 1963 Strat. "Her name's Mother," he told us. "And I'm very lucky to have her." Yet as commonplace as a fake battered Strat may be among the blues-rock fraternity, this one, like Sayce himself, is the real deal.

The only mods Philip has made to his mainstay are the two bridge saddles, the pots, the addition of a resistor on the volume circuit to retain treble when the volume control is rolled down, and Dunlop 6000 fret wire. The keen-eyed will have noted Mother's multicoloured flecks of paint finish, which Philip explains: "Back in the day, Fender painted them all sunburst and somebody would call up and say, 'We need a white one', so they'd just spray white over the Sunburst."

Sayce also has a 1962 Stratocaster with a round-laminated rosewood fingerboard, so he's well-placed to settle any disputes about the differences, if any, that maple and rosewood necks make to vintage Strat tone. "That '62 sounds more like a 1950s maple neck – it just has a woody twanginess to it... [due to the round-laminate rosewood 'board's fret tangs going into the neck itself]. It's because there's less rosewood. On the '63, too, there's not a lot of wood left on here, so these tangs are going far into the maple. It makes a difference – any slab 'boards I've played have been darker."

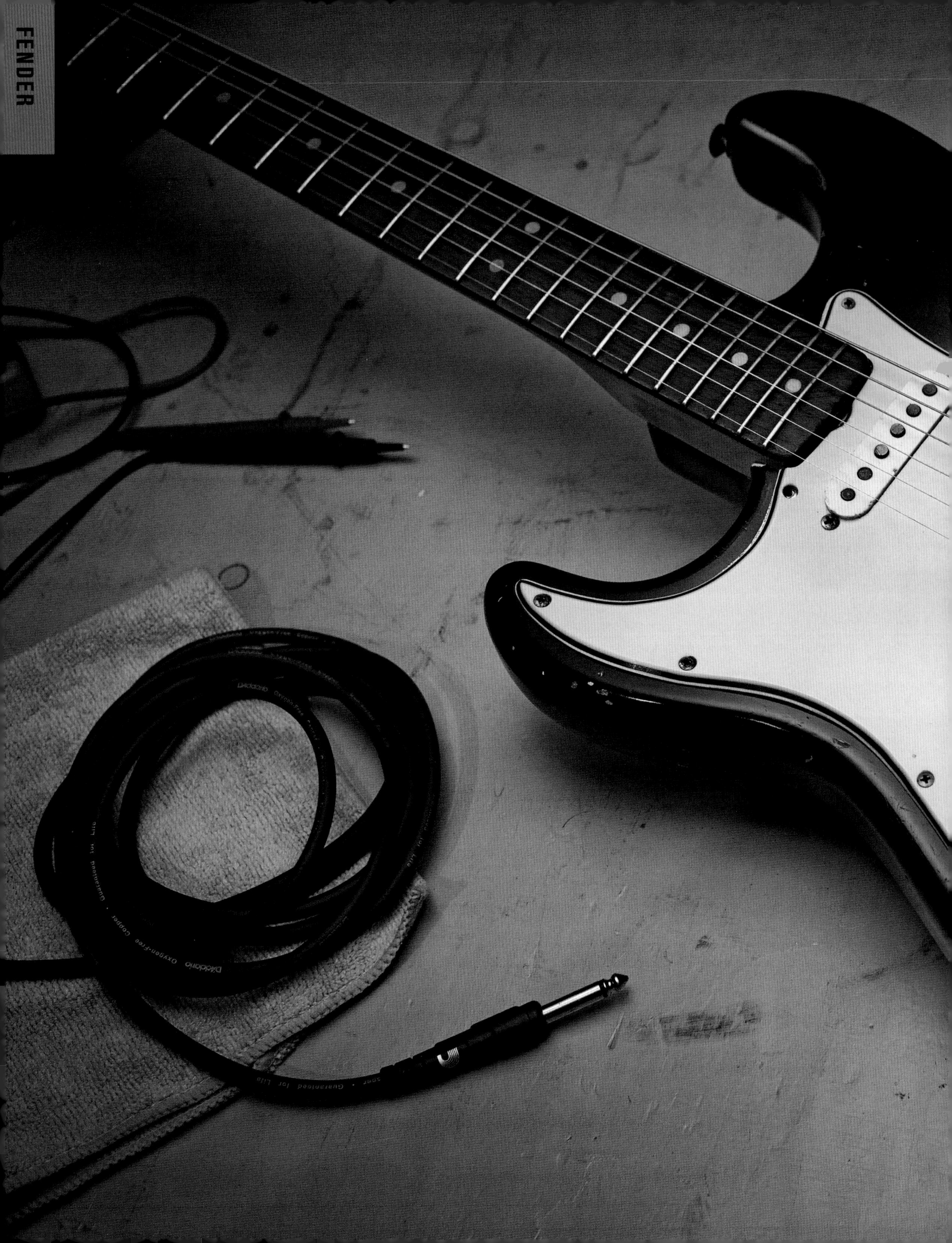
D'Addario Oxygen-Free Copper
Guaranteed for Life

FENDER

1964 L-SERIES STRATOCASTER

We all know that mid-60s Fender Strats are a rarity, but imagine the plight of a left-handed player trying to find one! This particular model, serial number L34810, left the factory in 1964 – the neck date is August of that year. Fender's L-Series serial numbers began to appear at the end of 1962, the company having exhausted the original system of sequential numbers by reaching 99999. Nicknamed 'Leo Models' by some, the L Series was comparatively short-lived, because when CBS bought the company in January 1965, serial numbers began to be prefixed with an 'F'.

Our super-rare model here is one of the last Strats to have the older-style sunburst finish; after this date the yellow in the sunburst became more opaque. As far as fixtures and fittings are concerned, it's pretty much what you would expect from a Stratocaster of this period. It's a medium to light weight with a fair but not excessive amount of knocks and bumps, five springs in the trem cavity and the usual amount of playing wear on the back of the neck.

FENDER

1965
CANDY APPLE RED
STRATOCASTER

Officially available in Fender's catalogue from 1963, Candy Apple Red quickly became one of the company's most popular colours. In fact, it's said that if you scratch the surface of a 60s Candy Apple Red Strat (hypothetically speaking, we're not advising you do so), you're likely to find a Sunburst finish underneath, as many guitars seem to have been resprayed this colour at the request of customers. After all, it was the 1960s and it seemed that everyone wanted a red Strat! Part of the allure of this custom colour was the fact that it was metallic, the finish being achieved by using a silver undercoat that was subsequently oversprayed with translucent red. A novelty, no doubt, in the decade that saw the Stratocaster's rise in popularity.

The other thing of interest here – certainly to the collector's market – is the transition logo on the headstock. With the sale of Fender to CBS in 1965, the new management decided to consolidate the logo, as they considered that there had been a confusing array of different designs up until that point. So graphic designer Robert Perine came up with that slightly larger, and considerably more legible, gold-outlined-in-black logo that was to sit atop headstocks until it was changed once again to the more familiar black '70s' type that was in use until the early 1980s.

Our sample here is in remarkably good condition for its age with very few battle scars in evidence. The nitro finish may have aged like it always does and some of the sparkle from the Candy Apple might have dulled, but we're betting that it sounds as good as ever!

FENDER

60TH ANNIVERSARY CLASSIC PLAYER 50S STRATOCASTER

Fender's Ensenada, Mexico-made Classic Player models are comfortably among the best-bang-for-buck Strats that money can buy, and for the Stratocaster's 60th Anniversary version in 2014, the Big F created a truly stunning value-for-money example. With its Desert Sand-finished ash body, gold-anodized aluminium pickguard, and maple vintage-meets-modern 9.5-inch radius neck, it's designed to turn heads; and hefty tones from that trio of American Vintage single-coils mean it'll capture hearts, too, especially if you're a player with blues-rock leanings. The Strat's enduring success is due in no small part to its reliability and capability as a no-nonsense gigging and recording guitar – and six decades on, the Classic Player Strat is an aptly named, shining example of its breed.

Custom Sh

LIMITED EDITIO

CUSTOM SHOP HEAVY RELIC STRATOCASTER

Who in their right mind would take a brand-new, Custom Fender Stratocaster, and beat it up to fake decades of wear and abuse? Well, Fender for one, and guitar players literally queue up to buy the results.

The concept is rumoured to have started in part via The Rolling Stones' Keith Richards who, on receiving a batch of new reissue Telecasters, bemoaned their 'newness' and asked Fender to "beat them up a bit."

The demand for 'Relic' guitars caught on, and Fender has been making more ever since. The two pictured here are 'Heavy Relic' variants. Updated with more 'modern' player-focused features like flatter-than-vintage fingerboards, bigger frets and bespoke pickups, they appeal to players who want the feel and look of an old guitar, without having to play it for 40 years.

—◦❦◦—

FENDER

AMERICAN VINTAGE STRATOCASTER

The electric guitar is a peculiar beast. All the 'best' ones were designed in the 1950s and 60s, they've barely changed ever since, and these exact designs are still used by the vast majority of top players the world over. Unfortunately, the genuine vintage ones cost a small fortune, so new 'reissues' offer a more affordable way into a new 'old' guitar. In 2012, Fender gave its American Vintage series reissue instruments a significant overhaul, going to town on all the tiny details and spec points that make them more period-correct than ever before. What emerged was an all-new '56, '59 and '65 Stratocaster with small yet significant differences to neck and body shapes, fingerboards, pickups, plastics and hardware. The American Vintage range has now been superseded by the current American Original range. If none of that means anything to you, enjoy a smug smile that you can save your cash and buy something far less expensive. For others, those tiny details mean absolutely everything…

TELECASTER

1951-54 TELECASTER

L eo Fender may have needed three goes at naming his initial electric guitar creation (Esquire, then Broadcaster), but he got everything else pretty much right first time. Introduced in 1950, the Telecaster was the pioneering mass-production solidbody. Simple construction kept costs down, but the end result was very effective, delivering bags of twang and sustain. This proved ideal for country music, Fender's initial target market, but over the past 50 years, the Tele has successfully seen service in just about every musical style imaginable.

Leo Fender was engineer first, designer second, and the Tele is all about function over form: and while it's comparatively short on curves and contours and high on hard edges and straight lines, many players prefer the no-nonsense Tele to its more streamlined stablemates. For the first four years, Leo clad his creation in butterscotch blond with a contrasting black pickguard; this marks out the most desirable examples, because blackguard Teles have assumed iconic status, helped by the patronage of Keith Richards, Bruce Springsteen and others.

FENDER

1952 TELECASTER

This seminal, world-changing icon of 20th century design didn't pick up its official name until 1952. In an oft-told tale, the original name in 1950 was 'Broadcaster', to which the Gretsch company objected as it owned a trademark on 'Broadkaster' for its drum line. The guitar briefly went nameless – aka 'Nocaster' – and was rechristened Telecaster in 1952, inspired by what was then the new television age.

Originals were ash-bodied with a single-piece maple neck and fingerboard. The bakelite black scratchplate earned the guitar its unofficial name – Blackguard – which this spec is referred to as to this day. Pickguards turned white in 1954, but the dear old Blackguard-spec Telecaster has remained among the most consistently popular instruments from the early 1950s to today.

An original example like this in good condition and with rock-solid provenance will set you back tens of thousands of pounds/dollars. It's a good job, then, that Fender makes much more affordable reissues.

FENDER

1953 TELECASTER

Following its evolution from the single-pickup Esquire – and despite Broadcaster naming wrangles – the Telecaster began life on the production line in February 1951. In its initial decade of production, some of the most intriguing changes took place within the guitar's control cavity. Initially, the pickup selector's bridge position activated both pickups, with the tone knob used to adjust the amount of neck mixed into the bridge-pickup sound – this was simplified in 1952 at guitarist Bill Carson's urging to output the bridge pickup on its own with tone control, as it is today. Meanwhile, the middle position delivered the neck pickup only with tone control, while the 'neck' position activated the neck with extra capacitance for a bassier tone and no tone control. This was the so-called 'dark' wiring format. This example, from the third year of production, has been modified for the control configuration that became standard in the late 1960s – bridge, both, neck. There's no doubt as to the circuit's origins, though: tucked inside the control cavity is a small piece of paper bearing the name 'Gloria', in reference to Gloria Fuentes, a Fender factory assembler who installed the pickups back in 1953. On the outside, this Tele is every bit the part, too, with a Butterscotch Blonde-finished ash body, black pickguard and trio of brass saddles, recalling iconic guitars of Bruce Springsteen et al. And as for the tone, it's wonderfully balanced in the neck and middle, with plenty of treble available from the bridge – it's good to know nothing's changed!

FENDER
1960-64
TELECASTER

An embargo on US-made imports after WWII meant Fenders weren't officially available in the UK until the start of the 1960s. By then, a rosewood fingerboard was standard, so we missed out on those lovely all-maple alternatives. The only other major change concerned the scratchplate, which switched to plain white in 1954, and then to a white laminate almost a decade later.

The Shadows ruled the roost in the UK at the time, and almost every player lusted after a Fiesta Red Strat. Lacking a third pickup and de rigueur wobbly bit, the Tele was regarded as a poor relation and tended to be relegated to rhythm, an image reinforced when Shadow-man Bruce Welch employed one for a short spell. However, players like James Burton, Steve Cropper and Pirates mainman Mick Green provided powerful proof that the Tele was certainly not strictly for strummers. Even so, a general lack of respect and its easily-stripped slab body made the Tele a prime target for modifying, which means all-original examples are now hard to find.

❧

FENDER

1968 TELECASTER

Generally speaking, the Tele has remained pretty faithful to its original design over the years, with many of the initial tweaks and modifications remaining hidden from sight. As an example, the very first models had no routing between pickup cavities, screws were changed from slot to Phillips head, decals moved, and other minor nips and tucks were to follow, but the Telecaster's basic essence remained pure throughout. A thoroughbred, two-pickup fireball that would eventually straddle the seemingly diverse worlds of blues, country, jazz and rock.

The 1968 model here may look Blonde at first glance, but we're reliably informed that it was once Olympic White – a colour prone to yellowing as it ages. Note how the fretboard wear is a virtual street map of the E minor pentatonic scale – rock 'n' roll!

FENDER

AMERICAN VINTAGE TELECASTER

Ever since the mid-1980s, Fender has offered a new 'reissue' version of a classic, vintage-spec Telecaster from its American production facility. While certain aspects of the original designs have been updated and 'improved' over the years in other Tele models (such as American Standard), the American Vintage Series instruments get ever more vintage-period-correct with each overhaul.

In 2012, Fender brought out all-new (old) '52, '58 and '64 reissue Telecasters with small yet significant differences to neck and body shapes, fingerboards, pickups, plastics and hardware. These subtle nuances will be all but lost on anyone but the most devoted of Tele fans, but to that exacting bunch, this level of detail makes the all-important difference.

American Vintage Teles use a nitrocellulose finish (cheaper Fender variants are usually polyester/polyurethane) that is more 'authentic' in terms of look, feel and the way it ages over time. More contentiously, many players also believe this kind of finish sounds better, too.

GIBSON

Gibson's historical product line contains an embarrassment of vintage riches. From curvaceous ES-175 jazz archtops, through seductive semi-hollowbody thinlines such as the ES-335, all the way to vintage guitar's Most Wanted, the 1959 sunburst Les Paul Standard – step this way to see some of the greatest Gibsons ever to leave Kalamazoo and Nashville.

GIBSON

BARNEY KESSEL CUSTOM

This signature model is a serious jazz guitar that's so sophisticated, it even has bowties for inlays.

Introduced in 1961 alongside a less ornate 'Regular' model, Gibson's Barney Kessels remained in production until 1973. The original 1961 list prices were $560 for the Custom and $395 for the Regular version. A longer heel with 14th-fret join was phased out by 1964, as you can see from this example, part of the collection at Guitars: The Museum in Umeå, Sweden. Physically huge with a long, Super 400-style headstock and a 17-inch lower bout, these instruments are wonderful jazz guitars, although Kessel appears to have favoured a 1940s Gibson ES-350 with a Charlie Christian pickup for stage and studio work. It may not have been the most enthusiastic of endorsements, but the Gibson BK guitars at least fared better than Barney's previous Kay signature models, of which he reportedly stated: "I don't play that Kay – it's a terrible guitar!"

✂

GIBSON

DWIGHT DOUBLE-CUT

Gibson's wildly successful Les Paul Junior inspired many variants, and here's one such rare 1960s example. The 1962 Dwight double-cut is one of only 75 guitars to bear the Dwight marque. They were made by Gibson for a US retailer, and were based on the Epiphone SB533 Coronet. Ultra-lightweight, with a single P-90, it's a stunning offshoot of the Junior design philosophy. This one is owned by XTC guitarist, Dave Gregory.

"I remember seeing Steve Marriott in Humble Pie with a little Dwight," Gregory explains. "I'd never seen one before. I learned later that they were a special order by this guy in St Louis, who had a shop called Sonny [Shields] Music." Here the double-cut is pictured left, alongside a 1961 SG/Les Paul Junior, right.

GIBSON
ES-175

Gibson's 1949 successor to the groundbreaking ES-150 was a runaway success, and the first Gibson electric to feature the Florentine cutaway: a sharp-pointed lower bout opening up access to all 20 frets. It originally came with a single P-90, then a two-pickup version appeared in 1953, followed by a twin-humbucker model in 1957. Its laminated top produced a bright, warm tone that's been used to fantastic effect by jazz greats such as Joe Pass, Steve Howe and Pat Metheny.

<figure>❦</figure>

GIBSON

STEVE HOWE'S 1964 ES-175D

Gibson's ES-175 debuted in 1949. The ES-175D (denoting its double pickup configuration) appeared four years later, and this particular specimen belongs to jazz great Steve Howe, who's owned it since the age of 17. "When it arrived, I remember plugging it into my Fender Tremolux and thinking, 'It sounds exactly like Kenny Burrell!'" Howe said. "I'd sit and listen to records just looking at it – almost meditating on it – and I played it as much as I could.

"I fitted a fancy inlaid bridge years ago, and these knobs are from a late-fifties guitar. I also got a [Kluson] machine head and whittled the tuning button down and fitted it as the pickup-selector toggle. It's had one re-fret, a couple of years ago, by Tim Stark at Manson Guitars. It's amazing that I let anybody do it, but it had a couple of buzzes in predictable places that I was tired of working around. But he did a brilliant job." This particular guitar is the personal property of Yes guitarist Steve Howe.

1958 ES-225T

An early thinline whose ephemeral production makes it a rare and sought-after vintage find.

It was in production for only a handful of years, but along with the Byrdland and ES-350T, the ES-225 was one of Gibson's first thinline hollowbodies when it launched in 1956. While its outline, complete with Florentine cutaway, was borrowed from the ES-175, its slimmer body depth made it a more comfortable proposition for players. The 225 offered different tonal possibilities, too, thanks to a single P-90, which – as on this example from Guitars: The Museum in Umeå, Sweden – was positioned between the bottom of the neck and the bridge, as opposed to the usual single-pickup bridge placement. Related ES-225TD models (1956-1958) featured a pair of P-90s in the usual positions, as on the recent reissue from Gibson Memphis. Aside from the glorious yellowed cream binding around the Sunburst finish, one of this 225's most eyecatching figures is the almighty wrapover 'bail' bridge and tailpiece, a similar configuration to P-90-equipped Les Paul Goldtops of the early 50s (but note the strings pass over the bar here), which has a slightly looser playing feel when compared with a typical tune-o-matic-style arrangement.

GIBSON
1961 ES-330

Gibson's ES-330 stands apart from the rest of the ES series like the 335, 345 or 355. Introduced in 1959, the 330 is a full hollowbody guitar, as opposed to its companion models that feature a solid centre block. But the differences don't end there, as the 330's neck joins the body at the 16th fret, as opposed to the 335, which joins at the 19th – at least, it did until 1969, when Gibson bowed to the weight of opinion among 330 players who felt that their upper fretboard access was impeded and put matters right by rejigging the neck joint to bring it in line with the rest of the range. The 330 also featured two P-90 pickups, as opposed to the 335's humbuckers. As rock 'n' roll took its hold on music's landscape and volume levels increased significantly, the 330's tendency to feed back became apparent. When we spoke to Jethro Tull's Martin Barre, he recalled buying a 330 in 1961 or '62 for the princely sum of £175: "As soon as the blues started rearing its head and people turned their amps up, it just didn't work. It howled!"

However, the 330 has had its admirers. Among the players who have succumbed to its charms are jazzers Grant Green and Emily Remler, as well as Radiohead's Thom Yorke and The Smiths' Johnny Marr. The model was discontinued in 1972, but has enjoyed the occasional reappearance in the Gibson Custom Shop's catalogue since. Our model here is from 1961, a year before the P-90s' plastic covers were replaced by the chrome variety. Judging by the obvious wear to the fretboard, this particular model has been well played during its 55-year lifetime – but, looking at the practically unmarked body, it's possible to assume that it has been well loved, too. (Guitar courtesy of Vintage Guitar Boutique, London.)

GIBSON
ES-335

When Les Paul created his famous 'Log' in 1941 – with its solid centre block and hollow wings to assimilate the look of a conventional archtop – he'd unwittingly laid the foundation for one of the most fabulously successful designs ever: the ES-335. Yet it was a full 17 years until the idea was fully developed, refined and realized, and only then as a response to the emerging rock 'n' roll sound.

Part of the reason for the 335's success was its playability. Unlike previous archtops, the neck joined at the 19th fret, giving superb upper-fret access, further aided by the double-cutaway body shape; it was also the first Gibson Thinline with 22 frets. Everyone from Chuck Berry and Freddie King to Eric Clapton, Larry Carlton, Ritchie Blackmore and Dave Grohl would fall under its spell.

The ES-345 debuted in 1959 – confusingly, the 355 was released after the 335 in 1958 – and presented an upgraded proposition. New stereo-output wiring intended for use with two amplifiers, and six-position Varitone switching for progressively changing the frequency emphasis were added.

The clash of the jazz archtop of the pre-war years with the new-fangled solidbody electric, and the demands of the new rock 'n' roll music were made manifest in the 335's design – and for 50 years and counting, it's been a storming success.

GIBSON
1958 ES-335

This used to belong to Larry DiMarzio. Extremely rare," says Samuel Åhdén of Guitars: The Museum, describing an instrument fit to make any self-respecting guitar addict weep with desire. Though the long pickguard extending past the bridge pickup was retained until late 1960, it's the lack of fingerboard binding that marks this particular guitar out as a dead cert early '58 example. The company shipped only 50 Natural models that year, with or without binding, so it's one of the rarest finds out there.

GIBSON

1968 ES-335 12-STRING

This sunburst specimen came to Bernard Butler by way of Johnny Marr, a fan of the rare 12-String 335. Butler, who burst onto the scene with Suede as one of the most exciting guitarists of the Brit Pop generation, has since established himself as a solo artist and an award-winning producer. He's also a guitar connoisseur, and when we caught up with him, he took us for a tour of his impressive collection, which included this ES-335 12-String.

"I went up to visit Johnny in 1995, and we played guitar together and watched Neil Young videos all night," Butler recalled. "Just before I left, Johnny said, 'I want to show you this,' and got out this 12-String. I told him I recognized it from The Smiths on *Top Of The Pops* and 'Sheila Take A Bow' and 'Shoplifters Of The World Unite' on *The Tube* in 1986; specific songs. He just said, 'I knew you'd know all that... so you take it'. Amazing, but Johnny's always so generous to me. We play very differently which, believe me, wasn't my intention when I started. This is the main guitar on The Smiths' 'Stop Me If You Think You've Heard This One Before', and I wrote [debut solo single] 'Stay' on it. A special guitar."

GIBSON

LUTHER DICKINSON ES-335

North Mississippi Allstars' guitarist Luther Dickinson wanted his signature 335's finish to mirror that of a vintage ES-175 owned by his father Jim, a renowned Memphis producer and musician, and the resulting dark sunburst with VOS patina is stunning. This is an instrument spec'd to deal with the thrills and spills of rock 'n' roll, and the aged Bigsby B7 vibrato and warm-toned Alnico II 'dog ear' P-90s contribute to a player's guitar that thrives on crunchy overdrive. The perfect foil for open tunings and slide work, this rootsy rebel is a seriously desirable variation on a timeless classic – availability is limited, however, so snap one up while you can.

GIBSON
ES-339

L et's get this straight – the ES-335 is a wonderful guitar. It's also fair to say that, measuring 16 inches at its widest point, it's significantly larger than, say, a Les Paul, which is enough to put some people off. Well, in 2007, Gibson's Custom Shop debuted the 14.25 inch wide ES-339 – a more compact and shorter alternative that retains many of the 335's best features, including its exceptional tone. Offered with two different neck profiles, and featuring a sidemounted jack socket and Gibson's clarity preserving Memphis Tone Circuit, the 339 is one of the best new Gibsons we've ever played.

⚜

1965 ES-345

Launched in 1959, the ES-345 was aimed to sit in between the 335 and the slightly more luxuriously appointed 355 models in the Gibson catalogue. Like its stablemates, the 345 was originally designed to summon up the mellowness of an f-hole jazzer and combine it with the raunch of a solidbody. In order to achieve this, the 335-style instruments had a maple block running the length of the body to add warmth and sustain as well as eliminate troublesome feedback in one fell swoop. One thing that set the 345 apart was its Varitone switching and stereo wiring, the former having achieved some notoriety in guitar circles, with many players insisting that it did more harm than good!

The model has seen some variations in its livery since introduction – for instance, on early models, the ring around the Varitone switch was black, with the upgrade to gold being introduced during the second year of production. The pickguard was also shortened in 1961 so that it no longer extended beyond the bridge and Gibson dropped the 'jazz style' tailpiece in 1982 in favour of the Les Paul-type 'stop' variety.

This gorgeous '65 Sunburst model features a single-bound rosewood fingerboard with double parallelogram inlays, a trapeze tailpiece with raised diamond motif, gold hardware, PAF pickups and the longer, non-rounded horns prevalent on the 60s 335 series. Notable ES-345 players include guitar connoisseur Steve Howe, who can be heard playing his Sunburst model on the Yes prog masterpiece, *Close To The Edge*.

1955 ES-350T

With one of these slick-playing hollowbodies in hand, Chuck Berry redefined rock 'n' roll.

In the mid-50s, Gibson decided to combat the solidbody guitar with a series of three guitars which, while still retaining some glitzy archtop features and styling, had thinner bodies and narrower necks with shorter 23.5-inch scales to enable easier chord stretches and faster lead lines. These were the budget ES-225T, the mid-range ES-350T and the Byrdland (so-called because it was designed in conjunction with Nashville session players Hank Garland and Billy Byrd).

The 1955 ES-350T, which we see here courtesy of Guitars: The Museum, has a figured maple body, P-90s and a rounded Venetian cutaway; specs were later updated with twin gold PAF humbuckers in 1957 and a curved Florentine cutaway in 1961, and the model was discontinued in 1963. Many famous players have favoured the ES-350T, but none have been more influential than Chuck Berry, who played one on his early era-defining recordings for Chess, including 'Maybelline' and 'Johnny B Goode'.

GIBSON

ES-355TDSV

Gibson's opulent semi-hollow ES-355TD was launched in the same year, 1958, as its more workmanlike sibling the ES-335, and was distinguished by more upmarket appointments including a multi-bound pickguard and top, triple-bound back, a bound ebony fretboard and split-diamond headstock. All of this added to an air of grandeur that made it, arguably, what the Les Paul Custom was to the Les Paul Standard: a more sophisticated big brother.

The ES-355 was initially launched as a conventional mono guitar, but the year after it made its debut, it received an upgrade that gave it the classic 355 spec. Initially offered as an option alongside the mono version, buyers of the ES-355 TDSV could route the output of the two pickups to separate amps, for a stereo rig – although this necessitated the use of a Y-cable. A more immediately obvious feature was the Varitone circuitry – essentially a series of notch filters, selected via a rotary switch that expanded the available tones on tap. Despite providing an extra bit of visual bling, however, most players would agree that the sounds offered by the Vari-Tone were of limited utility, and some 355 owners modify theirs to yield more usable variations. The sideways vibrato on this stunning 1962 example became standard-fit on all ES-355s from '61, the same year that the longer original pickguard was shortened to end above the bridge.

GIBSON
1951 ES-5

Back in its day, Gibson lauded its ES-5 as the "supreme electronic version of the L-5".

While the upstarts at Fender took a gamble on their futuristic new solidbody guitars, the Broadcaster and Esquire, Gibson's early 50s designs still evoked the golden age of jazz. Grand, glitzy and beautiful, the ES-5 is a perfect example of that design philosophy, with its 17-inch wide body and upmarket five-ply binding round the pointed-end rosewood 'board. This example, recently in stock at Vintage 'n' Rare Guitars in Bath, has a trio of P-90 pickups, each with its own volume control, while a single master tone knob is mounted on the cutaway bout. This unwieldy control layout was updated in late '55 to 'Switchmaster' spec, with the addition of dedicated tone controls for each pickup and a four-way switch. Plugged in, its old-school tone is glorious, with all that air inside adding a full but controllable bloom to each note. For such a grand-looking design, it's also surprisingly comfortable to sit and noodle with – the narrow-ish neck has a slender C-shape profile, and although the tiny frets don't encourage big bends, those Scotty Moore licks pop out like a charm. As hollowbodies from an earlier, grander era go, the ES-5 is a beauty.

GIBSON

EXPLORER

In 1957, Gibson was bridling at the success of Fender's futuristic Stratocaster, and decided to produce three outlandish models to beat its West Coast rival at its own game. The fabled Moderne fell by the wayside and became a Holy Grail of vintage guitar lore, but the two that made it into production – the Flying V and the Explorer – not only outgunned Fender in the crazy stakes, but they were also fantastic, enduring instruments in their own right... Eventually, anyway.

The V and Explorer may have been commercial failures, but they were avant garde concepts, and both would have their day. The Explorer's asymmetrical body, pointy headstock, and striking angles – not to mention its sustainful construction and chiming, powerful resonance – found plenty of admirers in the hard-rock fraternity of the 70s and 80s, Gibson duly fed the demand with a series of variations on the original theme. And once The Edge of U2 teamed his 1976 Explorer with a Memory Man and a Vox AC30 for hit after hit, the guitar's legendary status was assured.

GIBSON

FIREBIRD I

L ike the 'Modernistic' guitars before it, Gibson's Firebird was a determined response to Fender's dominance of the solidbody electric market – the company even approached a celebrated retired car designer, Ray Dietrich, to design it. Released in 1963, it was Gibson's first neck-through-body design, consisting of a nine-piece walnut and mahogany laminate running the length of the instrument, with a pair of thinner wings glued on to form the striking, lopsided parallelogram bodyshape. Though it owed something to the Explorer, the Firebird toned down that model's defiant angularity in favour of curvature, and added a complementary reverse headstock with banjo-style tuners.

The Firebird originally came in single, double and triple mini-humbucker options, and many different variants and body styles – reverse and non-reverse (introduced in 1965) – each of which has their own history and which look totally different. However, despite the many changes the Firebird ultimately failed to set the world alight. Over the years, however, its stock has risen, thanks in part to being seen onstage with the likes of Brian Jones, Johnny Winter, Eric Clapton and Phil Manzanera. Its original marketing promised "sharpness in the treble and deep, biting bass," a fair description. The Firebird's burning appeal continues to light up rockers young and, er, not so young!

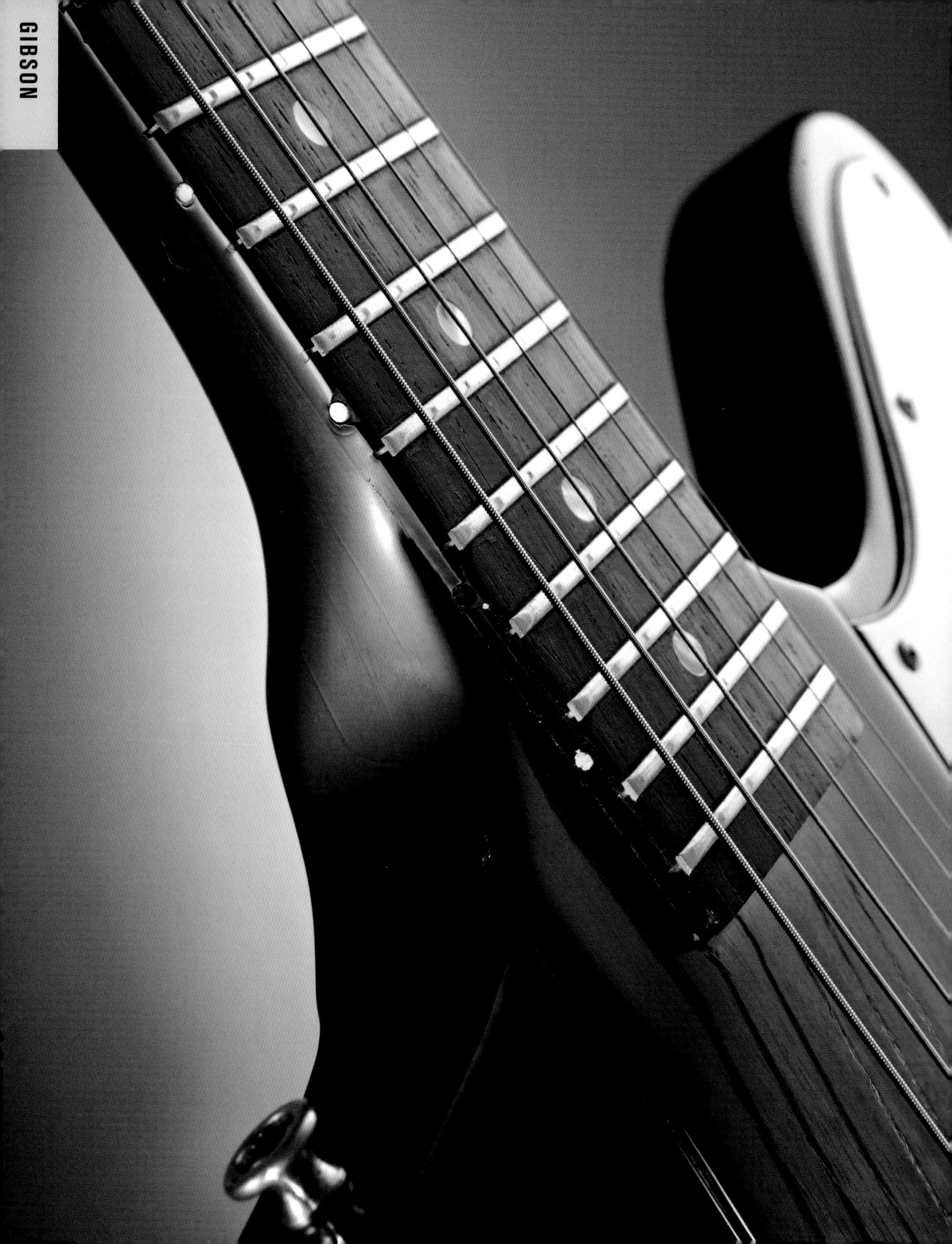

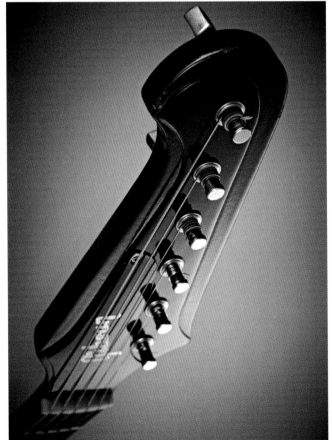

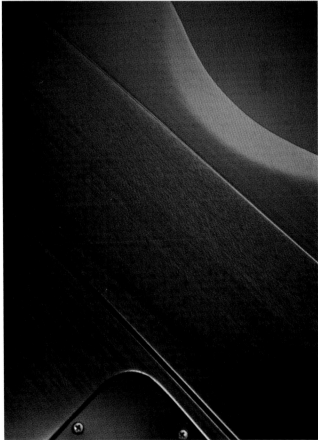

GIBSON

1967 FIREBIRD V 12-STRING

G ibson's Firebird was first launched in 1963 as a counter-attack on Fender's success with the Stratocaster and Telecaster. Gibson was currently witnessing a decline in its solidbody range, as the later phenomenal success of the Les Paul was still a few years in the future. Company president Ted McCarty tasked Ray Dietrich to come up with a revolutionary, modern-looking guitar and, no doubt inspired by the earlier Explorer and perhaps a cheeky nod to Fender's Jaguar and Jazzmaster, he came up with this distinctive body shape. Known initially as the 'reverse' model because of its extended treble-side horn and 'upside down' tuners, the Firebird enjoyed various spec and pickup configurations over the next few years, with the Firebird I bearing a single pickup, the III loaded with two, and the V including a vibrato and slightly more deluxe appointments. The design was also adapted for the Thunderbird II and IV basses, which entered the catalogue in 1963.

In 1965, Gibson introduced the non-reverse version of the Firebird, which saw the extended horn swapped to the treble side and this was to become the shape of the Firebird V 12-String we see here. To say that these 12s are rare would be an understatement – Gibson tells us that fewer than 300 were made during their '66/'67 period of manufacture. This model is finished in the extremely unusual Inverness Green custom colour, making it practically unique.

GIBSON

1964
FIREBIRD VII

Gibson's original Firebird's burned all too briefly in the company's catalogue, appearing in mid-1963 and disappearing again in May '65. At the time, its radical shape – both in reverse and non-reverse body guises – proved to be too much for the guitar-buying public, even though Fender's somewhat similarly space-age Stratocaster was rapidly finding its way into the hearts of players worldwide.

Blueprinted by car designer Ray Dietrich, who had both the Lincoln and Packard autos on his CV, the idea was that the Firebird's general appearance should reflect the tail fins of the 50s rides favoured by teenage rock 'n' rollers of the day. But this attempt on behalf of Gibson to get down with the kids floundered, and the guitar was consigned to the growing stockpile of six-string ideas that very nearly made it. However, Gibson's 'Bird wasn't going to go down without a fight; its solid mahogany neck-through body, Fender-ish six-a-side 'hawk's-head' headstock, Kluson banjo-style tuners and other features soon met the eyes of players who were looking for something a bit different, and the guitar began to enjoy a kind of posthumous fame. Arguably, it was Johnny Winter who led the charge, but players as diverse as Skunk Baxter, Elliot Easton, Eric Clapton, Mick Taylor and Dave Grohl were ultimately to succumb to its charms, and, today, the Firebird is highly regarded as an instrument that has risen, phoenix-like, from the ashes of a disappointing initial production-run to have its distinctive voice heard across the globe.

GIBSON

1958 FLYING V

This icon of the space age has held rock and blues players in its thrall for generations.

On its launch in 1958 as part of Gibson's Modernist Series, the Flying V shared a $247.50 price tag with the Les Paul Standard. Gibson's design chief and president Ted McCarty had begun developing prototypes the previous year, likely inspired by Cadillac tailfins and the Atomic Age optimism that fuelled a general enthusiasm for all things futuristic that even saw the Ford Motor Company design the Nucleon, a nuclear-powered concept car. Though the originals didn't sell in sufficient numbers to sustain initial production beyond 1959, artist association – Lonnie Mack, Albert King, Jimi Hendrix – and sheer cool would eventually help the V attain legendary status. With just 81 Flying Vs leaving the factory in 1958, this beautiful original model on display at Guitars: The Museum in Umeå is comfortably in the 'Burst bracket when it comes to monetary value.

GIBSON

FLYING V

The Flying V was the first of Gibson's Modernistic designs of 1958, and was the one that contrasted most decisively with the rest of the Gibson catalogue. Those early 1958 specimens are among the most collectible of all vintage guitars, and while guitarists of the future would embrace the V's awkward shape for all manner of styles, players of the late 50s were happier with their Les Pauls, Strats and Teles.

And yet, some influential name players spotted the V's potential. Lonnie Mack, Albert King and Dave Davies all made an early splash with one, and later in the 60s Keith Richards increased its notoriety. A second-run Flying V was Jimi Hendrix's blues guitar of choice – and almost every time you hear him tear through 'Red House', it's a Flying V he's using to redesign the blues. The 70s saw hard-rock players like the Schenkers gravitate towards the V; in the 80s, it was Metallica's Kirk Hammett and James Hetfield who harnessed it to their brutal ends, and the design spawned many reissues, variations – and imitators.

※

GIBSON
1952 L-5

Gibson's L-5 was first introduced in late 1922, the brainchild of the company's luthier, Lloyd Loar. Original pure acoustic models were 16 inches wide and sported a birch back and maple back and sides, single bound ebony fingerboard, dot inlays and a triple-bound peghead. The model underwent several upgrades, including gold-plated hardware, a maple back and block inlays. The most significant advances were the slight increase to body size, which occurred in 1934 when Gibson added an inch to the model's girth, and in 1939, when the model received a rounded cutaway and the model that we're familiar with today was born.

Renamed the L-5C, the guitar became a favourite among the big band jazzers of the 1940s, its unamplified volume and projection able to cut through the horn sections of the day. The first pickups to appear on the L-5 (now called the L-5 CES) were P-90s in 1951, which were upgraded to Alnico V pickups in 1954 and humbuckers in late '57. Further additions to the range were made in the form of the L-5 Studio and L-5S solid body, but the original CES still remains close to the hearts of modern day jazzers.

This Sunburst model is from 1952 and, we're told, is one of only 29 made in that year. It sports an almost regal charm and is a remarkably clean version of one of Gibson's landmark jazz guitars.

‒❧‒

GIBSON
1953 L-5 CES

Gibson's L-5 CES has an illustrious history. It began life as far back as 1922, when it originally featured in the catalogue as an acoustic archtop. It was also the first guitar the company made that featured f-holes, and went on to be number one on the list for big-band guitarists because of its big sound.

The first electric model came out in 1951, with a carved spruce top, maple back and sides and a pair of P-90 pickups, with these being upgraded to Gibson's Alnico V pickups in 1954, before humbuckers became the norm and an ABR bridge replaced the wooden one in late 50s.

Players of note who used an L-5 include Scotty Moore – you can see his blonde model in action in films of Elvis Presley's 1950s performances – and jazzer supreme, Wes Montgomery, who went on to have his own signature model based on the design.

Our model here is one of only 18 blonde L-5s that Gibson made during 1953 – although the presence of Alnico Vs here would suggest that it must have been late in the year – and shows very little evidence of wear. The spruce has mellowed down from blonde to amber with very few marks or blemishes, and there's little indication of any fretboard wear, either, suggesting that this is an instrument that has been used but well loved by its owners over the years. (Guitar courtesy of the New Kings Road Vintage Guitar Emporium.)

GIBSON

1950S LES PAUL 'GOLDTOP' ORIGINAL

Gibson's first Les Paul signature model, launched in 1952 (pictured), was a cocksure riposte to the emergence of Fender's 'plain' mass production electrics, the bolt-on Esquire and Telecaster. The Les Paul's carved top promised the hand-crafted allure of Gibson's best jazz guitars, while the rich colour positively screamed opulence – indeed, one of Paul's key inputs was to specify a gold-painted body ("it looks expensive"), and a mahogany fingerboard – ("it makes your fingers appear to move faster on the fretboard"). The whole, said Les, approvingly, "looks classy – like a tuxedo."

Tuxedo? Rock 'n' roll, the Goldtop was not. But rock 'n' roll didn't really exist back then. The original trapeze tailpiece didn't work too well, and was replaced by the tune-o-matic a few years later; the original neck angle was also too shallow for tuning stability; plus those single-coil pickups wouldn't have sated proto-rockers anyway. But undoubtedly, it's an icon; not only of all the following Les Pauls, but of 'special' guitar colours too.

In a post-war world, the Les Paul 'Goldtop' was electric guitar bling at its finest, and its rarity alone makes for huge prices: back at the height of the vintage boom, we found (claimed) originals offered for up to $24,000. Gold dust, indeed.

GIBSON

1958-60 LES PAUL STANDARD

A misnomer in retrospect, the '58-'60 Standard is now perceived as the most unique guitar in the collecting world. With Gibson consigning 'Goldtops' (for then) to history, in 1958 they settled on a new sunburst finish. Notably, the guitars' maple tops were now visible. The woods on some offered an almost-3D 'flame' or 'figure'; on others, the ultraviolet-sensitive dye of the tops faded in natural light, making for a more uniform yellow-ish brown – the 'sunburst' became what collectors now call 'unburst'. Either way, many pieces were – to a very keen eye – individual.

There were various minor changes in the guitar's short original life, such as fretwire, neck profile and jack plate, but the model wasn't at all popular at the time.

Its mellow/fat tones could be good for jazz: but jazz players generally preferred hollowbodies. And early rock 'n' rollers preferred the brighter tones of Fender's Strat and Tele. Hence, Gibson discontinued subsequently taking on the SG outline (until 1968).

Single-cut Les Paul Standards may have remained unloved too, but for the likes of Eric Clapton and Mike Bloomfield who revved them up in the mid-60s blues-rock explosion; to many, these white bluesmens' revival of the Standard's hidden potential kickstarted the whole 'vintage' guitar phenomenon we now know and love/loathe. Only 1,712 original 'sunburst' Les Pauls were made from 1958 to 1960, making those first Standards museum pieces. Maybe only 20 per cent had significant 'flaming' on their tops, but that just makes the prices worse.

The mojo-laden '59 owned by both Peter Green and Gary Moore was offered for sale for an incredible $2m.

GIBSON

1959 LES PAUL SPECIAL

Introduced in 1955 as a step up from the single-pickup Junior, the single-cutaway Les Paul Special was still considered a 'student' model, and priced accordingly. The double-cut incarnation arrived midway through '58, with the TV finish now distinctly yellow in hue. Gibson's November 1959 price list saw the Special cost $195, versus the $265 Standard, while the Custom topped the range at $395 ($470 with Bigsby). None of those prices included a hard case, which was an additional $42.50.

1959 saw the Special's pickup selector switch moved from its original position between the treble volume and tone pots and relocated closer to the bridge (as seen here), while just weeks after this example was shipped, neck pickups on new models were moved approximately half an inch closer to the bridge unit in order to strengthen the neck joint. The guitar pictured has a chunky D-shaped neck and bags of sustain and resonance. Don't believe the hype about wraparound bridges, either; the intonation is bang on!

GIBSON

1959 LES PAUL STANDARD

In the immortal words of Spinal Tap's Nigel Tufnel, "This is the top of the heap right here." Nobody would argue with him now, but in fact the Les Paul struggled for commercial success right from its launch in 1952. It acquired a new tune-o-matic bridge and stop tailpiece in 1955, new PAF humbucking pickups in 1957, and the almost last-ditch attempt to revive its fortunes came in 1958 with the sunburst finish. Evolution complete, it set the blueprint for what fans, collectors and pundits refer to affectionately as a 'Burst': a 1958-60 Les Paul Standard. Gibson records show that less than 650 Les Paul Standards were shipped in 1959.

Nevertheless, still 'unpopular', it was ingloriously replaced in 1961 with the pointier, thinner Les Paul shape which we would later come to know better as the SG. Then in 1965, Eric Clapton played a 'Burst on the 'Beano' album with John Mayall's Bluesbreakers, as did Michael Bloomfield with the Paul Butterfield Blues Band in the USA, both helping to reignite the guitar's fortunes, and beginning a 'vintage' obsession with the model that continues unabated to this day.

This incredible, original 1959 example is 'The Beast', owned by ex-Whitesnake man Bernie Marsden.

REISSUE 1959 LES PAUL STANDARD

What do you mean, you don't have a quarter of a million for an original 1959 'Burst? Fear not, because since 1993, Gibson has been making ever more vintage-accurate 1959 Les Paul Standard reissues.

In 2013, the whole Gibson Custom range underwent a series of spec updates including the use of Aniline dyes (that give a very specific hue to the backs and necks) and a hot hide glue neck joint. In addition to the myriad period-correct features Gibson has been perfecting over the years, this is the closest new guitar to an original '59 Standard that you can buy officially.

You'll see these guitars referred to as 'R9', which simply means 'Reissue 1959'; likewise, the 1958 Reissues are referred to as 'R8'. There are two main differences between the two: 1959 Les Pauls tended to have slightly slimmer (though by no means slim!) necks, and more extravagantly figured maple tops.

GIBSON

1960 LES PAUL STANDARD

The 1958–1960 Gibson Les Paul Standard has since become – through a combination of its utility, rarity, market hype and simply by being in the right players' hands at the right time – the Holiest of vintage Holy Grails. This 1960 model from the Guitars: The Museum collection shows precisely why the hype (if not the crazy pricetag) is justified in the minds of guitar nuts everywhere.

Even in today's relatively chastened vintage market, you'd still expect to pay a six-figure sum to feel the weight of its 'Burst mahogany body and the drive of its PAFs: but then, it is the same historic tone that the likes of Eric Clapton, Peter Green and Keith Richards redefined blues and rock guitar with, and how do you place a value on that?

GIBSON

COLLECTOR'S CHOICE #18 'DUTCHBURST' 1960 LES PAUL STANDARD

Gibson's Collector's Choice series presents limited-edition recreations of specific '58 to '60-era instruments. The woods used are as near-perfect a match as possible to the originals, and the specific instrument this 'Dutchburst' is modelled on was bought in the Netherlands by a professional guitarist (we know him only as 'Jan'), who played jazz in his trio, mainly on cruise ships.

Gibson has recreated the years of wear and tear obsessively, although the finish is less dulled than on most VOS models. Its moody 'tobacco fading to burnt umber and caramel' finish is complemented by its tones, coming courtesy of period-correct Scatter Wound Custom Buckers, and sonically, all the usual quality Les Paul clichés apply. According to Les Paul aficionado and former guitar repairer for Gibson, Neville Marten, Ol' Dutch is "expressive, dynamic, woody, powerful-but-not-mushy, bright-but-not-piercing… If you're a guitarist who gets the whole vintage thing, a guitar like this is a joy to behold, a thrill to play and exhilarating to hear." High praise indeed.

GIBSON

LES PAUL CUSTOM

It stands to reason: if you have a 'Standard', then you need a 'Custom'; a higher-spec guitar for which you can charge a premium. And so it was in 1954, when Gibson prototyped a Les Paul with an upmarket, all-black finish and bound-headstock. More significant was the introduction of the all-new tune-o-matic bridge and stop tailpiece that enabled individual-string adjustment, plus lower, wider frets requested by Les Paul himself, leading to one of the guitar's nicknames, the 'Fretless Wonder'. Many people prefer 'Black Beauty'.

An ebony fingerboard helped give the guitar a slightly brighter tonality than the Standard (which uses rosewood), but the Custom's overall spec has changed significantly over the years. Bodies have been made either all-mahogany, or mahogany with a maple cap and there have been both two- and three-pickup models. Likewise, necks have been both solid mahogany or a mahogany/maple laminate depending on year. Gibson continues to produce reissues of the model to this day.

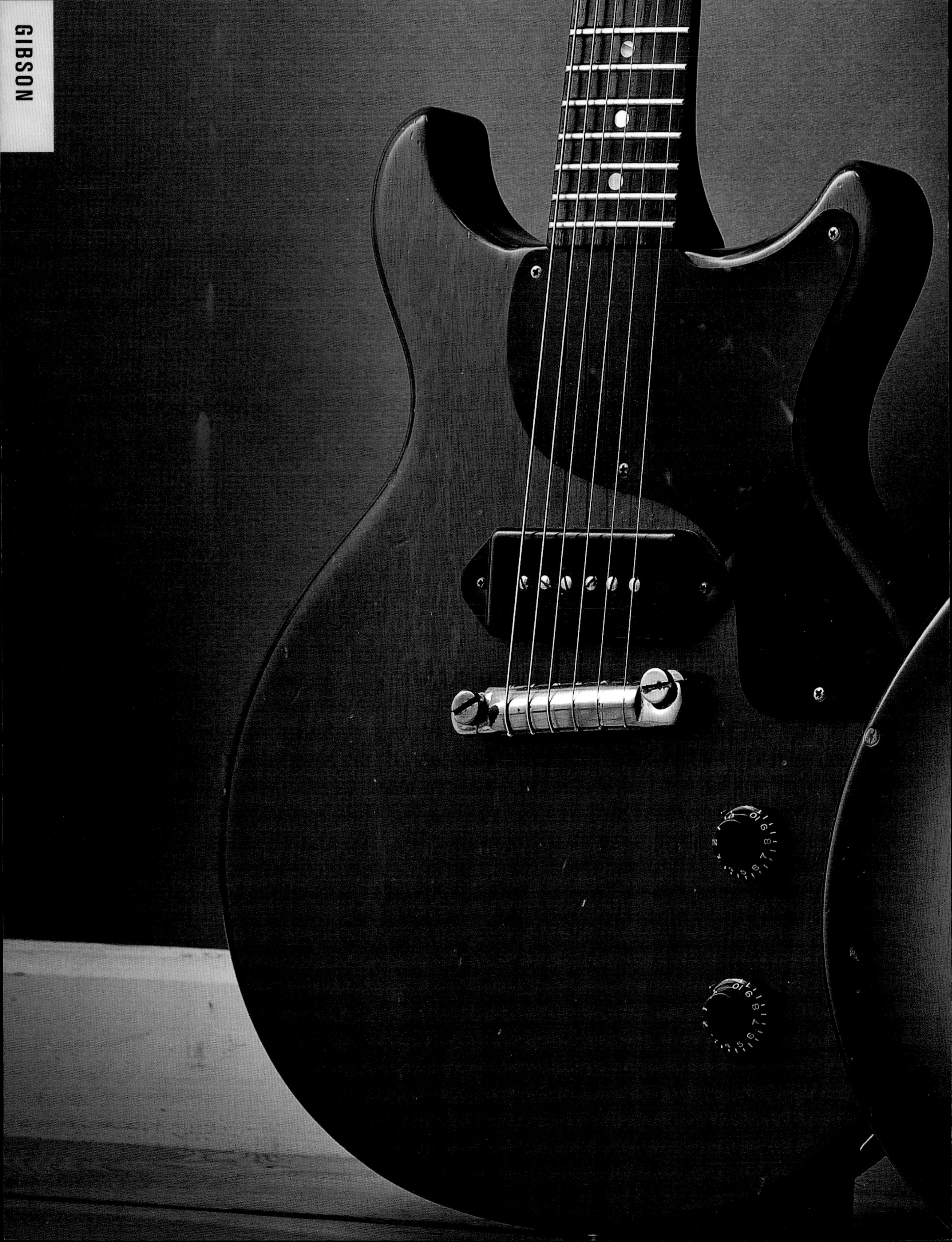

GIBSON

LES PAUL JUNIOR

Gibson's mid-50s student version of the Les Paul was based on a disarmingly practical concept. Simply remove all the stuff that makes Les Pauls expensive to produce – eg, the carved maple top, the binding, the extra P-90 – and sell the resulting guitar more cheaply.

The Junior's no-nonsense attitude extended to its tone and playability. A single P-90 with a single tone and a single volume control may sound limiting, but its fans – including John Lennon, Bob Marley, Johnny Thunders, Leslie West, Peter Frampton and Billie Joe Armstrong – are a diverse bunch, attracted like moths to a TV Yellow flame by the driving directness of its sound.

The single-pickup Junior was joined a year later by the twin-pickup Special, and in 1958, Gibson changed the body to a fragile twin-cutaway design which presaged the Gibson SG. Original Juniors are a find on the vintage market; but ultimately, they're a workhorse to be played and abused, not collected and hoarded.

GIBSON

1957 LES PAUL JUNIOR

Players from Leslie West to John Lennon have been drawn to the incisive tone of this Gibson student model. Released in 1954 alongside the more upmarket Les Paul Custom, Gibson's Les Paul Junior was aimed squarely at the budding student-guitar market of 1950s America. Its flat (not carved) singlecut body sported a lone P-90 pickup, and a list price of $99 – less than half that of the Goldtop – made it the best-selling electric of 1955. Its simplicity appealed to successive generations of rock players, among them Dave Gregory, formerly of XTC and the owner of this prime example, who was inspired to buy it after seeing Mountain's Leslie West riffing with his: "When I got it, sure enough there was Leslie, fast asleep in this guitar," he told us.

❦

1961 LES PAUL (SG) JUNIOR

In 1961, Gibson was busy transforming its entire Les Paul line, ostensibly to revive interest in its solidbodies, but also, it seems, to completely confuse future guitar historians. As well as radically transforming the bodyshape of the flagship models into what we now naturally think of as the SG shape, the company applied its new ultra-slimline doublecut body design to the Les Paul Junior, to the SG TV, to the SG Special, and to the SG Special Three-Quarter. During 1963, Gibson then proceeded to drop the Les Paul name from the redesigned Junior, and in its catalogues and other promo material, gradually renamed it the SG Junior.

This lone-P-90-toting 1961 SG-shape Les Paul Junior is owned by Daniel Steinhardt, founder of TheGigRig. "They're surprisingly versatile," Daniel told *Guitarist.* "I've used mine with Marshall Plexis, a Tweed Deluxe, Vox AC30, and it brings something to them all. They're remarkably full-frequency and resonant: whether you're just using the guitar to push the amplifier or whether you're using pedals into a very open-sounding amp, Juniors just work."

❊

GIBSON

1967 MELODY MAKER

Gibson first introduced the Melody Maker into its catalogue in 1959. Initially, it had a body shape similar to that of the Les Paul Junior, but was slightly thinner, and featured a simple inventory including an all-mahogany build, a single pickup, wraparound bridge/tailpiece, controls mounted on the pickguard and an unbound neck with dot inlays. It was aimed at being a no-frills budget model in counterpoint with Gibson's prestige electrics, such as the ES and Les Paul ranges. Things were set to change, however, and the body shape underwent several redesigns during the 1960s. By 1961, for instance, the Melody Maker had a double-cutaway and a year later was offered with an optional Maestro tremolo. Our model here represents possibly the most radical change: an SG-type double-cut – introduced in 1965 – with three single-coil pickups and a tremolo, possibly a reaction to the burgeoning popularity of Fender's Stratocaster. Nicknamed the Melody Maker III, the pickups were high output, with a three-way selector switch mounted on the lower horn.

The colour of the '67 is another rarity; the SG-shaped Melody Makers usually came in either Fire Engine Red or Pelham Blue, but this is the unusual metallic custom colour, Sparkling Burgundy, making this particular instrument of great interest to the collector market.

GIBSON
SG

Sister Rosetta Tharpe, Eric Clapton, Pete Townshend, Tony Iommi, Angus Young, Frank Zappa, George Harrison, Mick Taylor, Robbie Kreiger, Derek Trucks, David St Hubbins... The SG – née Les Paul – has proved itself time and again as the go-to guitar for exhilarating, high-energy rock, inventive psychedelia, and heavy blues. It's survived mid-60s stylistic tinkering, 70s corporate meltdown and 80s metal-driven excess, and still guitarists flock to it.

Perhaps it's the ease of access provided by the twin-horned double cutaway; the simplicity of the setup; the 'alternative' persona; the light weight or the demonic vibe. Whatever the secret ingredient that makes them endure, just know this: you haven't lived until you've windmilled open G, D, E and A, really loud, on an SG.

GIBSON
SUPER 400

Taking pride of place in Gibson's archtop lineage, the regal Super 400 was introduced with a fanfare in 1935 as the "biggest, fanciest archtop ever built". Like many early Gibsons, its model number was an indication of its price – and despite the big bucks needed to secure one, the Super 400 soon became a premier jazz box du jour. Unlike the plain-Jane L-5, its supersized 18-inch-wide multi-ply body was adorned with an engraved tailpiece and a mother-of-pearl headstock, with liberal use of binding.

1939 saw the first of some significant changes: an enlarged upper bout and f-holes, an L-5-like tailpiece and a Venetian cutaway, and 1940 saw a construction change from X- to parallel bracing, altering the character of its warm and resonant sound. War halted production for a decade, and after it was reintroduced in 1949, the Super 400 evolved further to include an electric version, the CES: it remains in the Gibson catalogue in this format to this day.

GORDON SMITH
GS2 60

The UK's longest-running guitar maker is criminally overlooked – and guitars like this GS2 60 are the indisputable proof. Gordon Smith's guitars such as the one pictured were hand-made in Partington, near Manchester, and offer a credible alternative to the more famous American brands. All GS's instruments are realistically priced and also offer a range of options to further tailor the guitars to your tastes and requirements.

This GS-2 is a Melody Maker-esque singlecut with a Brazilian cedar body. Its cedar neck has a shallow C profile to its rosewood 'board, medium-jumbo frets, simple pearloid dot markers and, unusually, it incorporates a height-adjustable brass nut.

Its GSG humbuckers are coil-splittable, and impart a classic, timeless rock tone with versatile sonic options. If you fancy something a little different from the norm and want good quality with a sensible price tag, you should seek out a Gordon Smith – now made under the same name by new owner, Higham Ferrers – with all due haste.

GRETSCH

1957 CHET ATKINS COUNTRY GENTLEMAN

C het Atkins' association with Gretsch began in 1954 with the introduction of his Hollow Body guitar, which was subsequently renamed the Nashville 10 years later. But possibly the most famous project he embarked on with the company came to fruition in 1957, with the issue of the Country Gentleman. Initially, Chet had wanted a centre block for his new model, as featured in Gibson's semi-hollow guitars, but Gretsch had other ideas and went for a totally hollow body, to the delight of contemporary Gretsch collectors everywhere who are fearful that a centre block would have produced a very different-sounding guitar. Gretsch got around the problem of feedback at volume by plugging the f-holes with plastic inserts, as featured on the instrument here, but on later models they were painted on.

Chet also wanted a wide neck, so this model features a five-piece neck, something that was abandoned very early on in production. In fact, it's thought that only 15 or so wide-neck models were ever made. The pickups are of significant interest as they predate the more familiar Filter'Trons; these are pre-patent "Smooth'Trons", as they are known among collectors. It's said that Ray Butts was neck-and-neck with Gibson in the development of the humbucking pickup, but Gibson was first past the post with the PAF.

Other features include a brass nut, another of Chet's requests, but it was replaced with a bone nut and zero fret combo in 1959. Gretsch's flagship guitar not only found fame in its designer Chet Atkins' hands, when George Harrison was seen playing one on *The Ed Sullivan Show* in 1964, sales were given a massive boost!

GRETSCH

1960 6118 DOUBLE ANNIVERSARY

This 75th anniversary model was a fairly affordable guitar. Here's one with a difference (or two). Back in 1959, Gretsch was celebrating its 75th anniversary, but rather than issue a high-end creation to commemorate the occasion, it unveiled the affordable Anniversary model, which came in one- and two-pickup configurations. This example is the 6118, known as the Double Anniversary thanks to its Patent Applied For Filter'Tron humbuckers, which were replaced by HiLo'Tron single coils in 1961. The 6118 came in a desirable Two-Tone Smoke Green (inspired by Cadillacs from that era), and carried a luxurious 'Anniversary Model' nameplate on the headstock. The model's unbound ebony fingerboard and minimal control layout were basic compared with other models, but this guitar's previous owner made a few upgrades, replacing the G-cutout tailpiece with a Bigsby, while the presence of one selector switch and five knobs – as opposed to dual selectors and three knobs – makes us wonder if internal alterations took place, too. Along with the clear replacement pickguard, this guitar's other idiosyncrasy is the sticker near the base of the body – while this example won't win points for period-correctness, there's no denying the sheer cool emanating from those f-holes.

GRETSCH
1954 6120

Although Gretsch can boast arguably the most sought-after vintage guitar of them all – the ultra-rare 1958 PX6134 White Penguin (originally listed at $490) can be yours for a mere £40,000 or more – it's the Southern-fried 6120 that will surely remain at the top of any Gretsch collector's tree. Colloquially referred to as the Nashville, it was initially released in late 1954 as the Model 6120 Chet Atkins Hollowbody, priced at $385. The body was 15.5-inches deep, and therefore offered what Gretsch proclaimed was "a new look".

There have been many re-releases of both original and streamlined specs, examples of the latter being the numerous Brian Setzer signatures. Vital characteristics of originals to look out for include various stylized Western-themed accoutrements such as a steer's head rather than horseshoe headstock inlay, the so-called cows-and-cactus fingerboard livery and a gold-plated B-6 Bigsby vibrato complete with a fixed rather than bent arm. Look out for DeArmond single coils and a 'signpost' scratchplate, too.

Models from 1957 demonstrate an overly scarlet hue to the curly maple body, but guitars from 1954 to 1956 are much more likely to exhibit what most of us would consider a classic, and thus more valuable, finish; that of Amber Red, commonly described as Western Orange.

GRETSCH

1967 6122 COUNTRY GENTLEMAN

Portishead's Adrian Utley is a jazz-trained guitar player and ambitious composer whose work calls for a diverse sonic palette. His 1967 Gretsch Country Gentleman (similar in spec to the one played by George Harrison on *The Ed Sullivan Show* in 1962, and the SuperTron-loaded variant once favoured for live use by Elvis as well as Stone Roses' guitarist John Squire) is a 1967 model, for studio use only; note the painted-on f-holes. These were incorporated onto the bound mahogany body at the request of the guitar's endorser, Chet Atkins, as a way of increasing sustain and reducing feedback.

GRETSCH

1958 6129 SILVER JET

There are cool guitars, and there are cool guitars. And then there's the Gretsch 6129. Introduced in 1954 as a variation on the 6128 Duo Jet, the Silver Jet sported a silver sparkle top derived from the plastic wrap that the company also used as a drum shell finish. Despite solidbody appearances, the instruments featured chambered two-inch deep mahogany bodies, while other specifications evolved rapidly throughout the first few years of production. This example, shot while on sale at Vintage 'n' Rare Guitars in Bath, likely dates from the first half of 1958. It sports the thumbnail fretboard inlays introduced early that year, but not the Filter'Tron pickups that later became standard issue. As you might expect with any 56-year-old instrument, this Silver Jet requires a little fettling to keep in tune, but the sound from those DeArmond Dynasonic single coils is truly monstrous; a twangsome thing of wonder and a killer rock 'n' roll machine.

GRETSCH

1965 G6120 CHET ATKINS

Manic Street Preachers' frontman James Dean Bradfield is a true gear lover, and typically takes 15 guitars with him on a full tour to take care of different tunings and, we suspect, just because he can. He's most linked in fans' minds to the white 1990 Gibson Les Paul Custom that's been on every album throughout the Manics' stellar career; but when we interviewed him in his 'Faster' Studio in Cardiff, he showed us some other gems from his guitar collection – including this beautiful 1965 Country Gentleman.

"It was bought from Fat Rick's Guitar Emporium just before *Everything Must Go*," Bradfield told us. "I used a Vox AC30 a bit more on that album and this Gretsch, and it really helped what I was trying to achieve, guitar-wise. It's also all over *This Is My Truth...* and *Journal For Plague Lovers*. It's the guitar on 'Your Love Alone Is Not Enough'. But on that track it's this Gretsch through a Marshall JCM900 linked up with a Diezel VH4. I was surprised how a hollowbody like this could sound so powerful, yet still have such a lovely colour-range across the strings.

"A lot of people seem to play Gretsches through quite boutique-y amplifiers, but they sound great through Marshalls or a Diezel, believe me. It's a star-spangled sound."

GRETSCH

1974 G7620 COUNTRY ROC

In the late-60s and early-70s, guitarists were beginning to feel disgruntled with their lot. Many felt the current production models of the day were inferior to guitars of the 50s and early 60s – partly owing to widely criticised buyouts of Fender by CBS and Gretsch by Baldwin – and this spearheaded what we now know as the vintage guitar movement. Gretsch picked up on the trend, introducing a number of new models with a distinct Western theme that evoked the Round Up models of the 50s, starting with the Roc Jet in 1969, then the Country Roc in 1974.

This 1974 Country Roc shows that Gretsch certainly went all out in re-embracing cowboy culture. Visual appointments include a 'G' brand on the top of the semi-solid body, studded leather around the sides of the guitar, a 'G'-cutout tailpiece with belt buckle, and even horseshoes on the bound ebony fingerboard's inlays and headstock. Pickups, meanwhile, were Super'Tron humbuckers, which were a little hotter than Gretsch's usual Filter'Trons. The Country Roc was only around for seven years, with production ceasing in 1979, but its introduction is significant, highlighting the growing feeling of nostalgia for the electric guitar's 'golden era' – something that has only escalated in the years since.

GRETSCH

1955 ROUND-UP

As corny as it looks by modern standards, the cows, steers and cactii that make up this 1955 Round-up's Western iconography were in keeping with many products of the day in the US. Designed to appeal to players in the burgeoning country and western scene, the single-cut Round-up was a high-end product in Gretsch's four-strong Jet line, and came loaded with a pair of DeArmond pickups for the requisite twang. It wandered off into the sunset in the late-1950s; if you want to lasso one yourself today, expect to pay a considerable sum for an immaculate specimen.

GRETSCH

WHITE FALCON

In 1954, screen siren Marilyn Monroe's skirt may have been fluttering in the updraft of a New York subway grating, but for US guitar players, it was a very different, yet equally voluptuous blonde that was infiltrating their dreams. Initially intended as a purely promotional item, the Gretsch 6136 White Falcon caught the eye at the NAMM trade show to such an extent that the company put it into production the following year.

Heralded as one of Gretsch's 'Guitars Of The Future', the hollowbody White Falcon was, is and always will be an expensive luxury item. Its (now) retrofuturistic allure is based on the automotive stylings of the 50s era down to its 'Cadillac G' tailpiece, and despite its large 17-inch lower bout, its popularity has endured despite the ineluctable trend towards smaller and more manageable instruments. This one sports a pair of Filter'Tron humbucking pickups, introduced in 1958.

GRETSCH

1958 WHITE FALCON STEREO PROTOTYPE

The White Falcon first entered the Gretsch catalogue in 1955 with the model number 6136 – a 431.8mm (17-inch) wide archtop with luxurious, gold-plated hardware set against its Snow White finish. Three years later a Stereo model appeared – the 6137 – with some cunning under-the-hood wiring and a dedicated amplifier and speaker system. But the model we have here is a real rarity because it is a prototype for the Stereo version, caught on an experimental cusp between models. "You can tell by the label '6136', which was the number for the Falcon, and it's been hand changed to '6137'," Phil Carwardine from Vintage And Modern Guitars tells us. "It got converted to mono sometime in the 60s, because the pot that has been changed from a switch is dated '66."

Of the unique wiring that Gretsch employed for the Stereo version, Phil says: "It would have been one pickup out of one amp and one pickup out of the other amp and then you could split the bass strings and the treble strings out of different amps, which I think wasn't that successful as you can probably imagine. It came with a load of satellite amps and I mean not just two, it was a bit like modern surround sound. It had a woofer, satellites and two big ones and it had a splitter box."

Indeed, the dedicated amp and speaker setup for the 6137 was a little cumbersome and it's no surprise that it didn't catch on with the guitarists of the day. The instrument itself, however, found a few fans: "The most famous fan is Neil Young with his Stereo Falcon. He did that charity gig [Farm Aid 2010] and it's just him solo playing 'Ohio' and he's got it set up for stereo and it just sounds incredible."

GUILD

STARFIRE IV

After a decade spent scared and discontinued, alone in the wilderness of eBay falling prey to savvy guitar hunters, Guild's back catalogue of electric guitars was finally resurrected and updated by owners Fender back in 2013.

Among the eight new models was the semi-hollowbodied Starfire IV, a child of the mid-1960s built for free love – or more accurately, freedom from hum and feedback. Though superficially similar to the ES-335 it was intended to compete with, it does have some telling differences –among them a mahogany top, distinctive voicing courtesy of the Guild 'Anti-Hum' Dual Coils and a floating bridge. Capable of transporting you anywhere from Swinging London to the Pacific North West garage scene, this relatively inexpensive Korean-made slice of doublecut retro nostalgia is also versatile enough to travel further forward through time, to handle late-60s psychedelia and edgier rock styles with ease.

GUS

G1 PURPLE SPECIAL

This design by Simon Farmer at Gus Guitars is fit for a Prince – the artist who inspired its striking looks. Its Red Western cedar core is covered with carbon-fibre laminate just 2.5mm thick; Simon then uses a coat of chrome-finish carbon fibre that allows him to apply the wonderfully over-the-top purple hue, before all metalwork is plated with genuine 22 karat gold.

It's no mere 'video' guitar, either. Playability is out of this world – the carbon-fibre board is nearly frictionless – while the mix of available tones from the custom-built pickups is truly expansive. Gus will build you a Purple Special at a pretty penny, but if you fancy something less, well, purple, the regular G1 range also offers this pioneering level of design and craftsmanship. Truly individual guitars: wonderful.

HARMONY

H54 ROCKET

Harmony's 1959 Rocket was a 20-fret student hollowbody that achieved widespread popularity through stylish looks, quality pickups and a keen price. There were three ultra-thinline Rockets in the range; the single-pickup H53, the dual 'Golden Tone' pickup H54 and the H59, loaded with three DeArmond 'Gold Tone Indox' pickups. Later variants on the H59 had creative approaches to control layout, with as many as six dials in a row, plus a rotary switch, competing for their player's attention on stage. This twin-pickup H54 Rocket is often used live by its owner, Adrian Utley of Portishead.

HARMONY
1963 H75

At its peak, Harmony was the largest musical instrument manufacturer in the USA. Founded by Wilhelm Schultz in 1892, it was later, under the ownership of Sears, Roebuck & Company, that the marque's appeal mushroomed as it made hay from Roy Smeck signature models, despite the backdrop of the Great Depression. 350,000 Harmony instruments with various brand names were sold between 1964 and '65 and the guitar pictured, armed with a trio of DeArmond 'Gold Foil' pickups, is typical of that era, though its original Sunburst finish has been stripped.

Dan Auerbach's use of the Bigsby-equipped version, the H78, has played no small part in transforming Harmony guitars of the period from forgotten pawn shop curios into sought-after cult classics for those of a dirty garage blues and indie persuasion. This particular instrument resided until recently at Vintage 'n' Rare Guitars in Bath, but if you can't find a vintage example there's always Eastwood's Airline-branded tribute model. Gold Foil single coils are also enjoying something of a renaissance, with pickup gurus such as Jason Lollar in the US and Mojo Pickups in the UK making great-sounding aftermarket replicas of vintage Teisco units. None-more-boutique Texan maker Collings even had a Gold Foil-loaded guitar on its stand at the NAMM show...

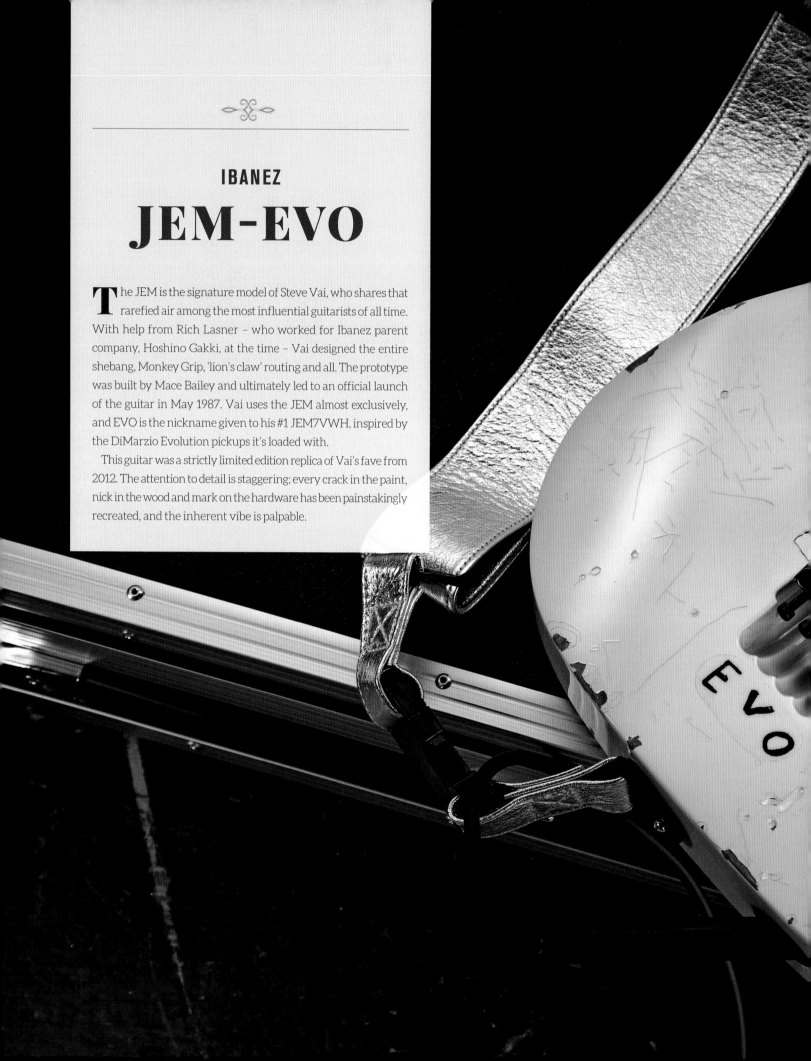

IBANEZ

JEM-EVO

The JEM is the signature model of Steve Vai, who shares that rarefied air among the most influential guitarists of all time. With help from Rich Lasner – who worked for Ibanez parent company, Hoshino Gakki, at the time – Vai designed the entire shebang, Monkey Grip, 'lion's claw' routing and all. The prototype was built by Mace Bailey and ultimately led to an official launch of the guitar in May 1987. Vai uses the JEM almost exclusively, and EVO is the nickname given to his #1 JEM7VWH, inspired by the DiMarzio Evolution pickups it's loaded with.

This guitar was a strictly limited edition replica of Vai's fave from 2012. The attention to detail is staggering; every crack in the paint, nick in the wood and mark on the hardware has been painstakingly recreated, and the inherent vibe is palpable.

IBANEZ

RG550

Released in 1987, in the same year as the Steve Vai-endorsed JEM, the RG550 was a similarly equipped beast featuring a new streamlined body with HSH configuration, 24 frets, and Ibanez's super-slim Wizard neck profile. Built for speed, it became an all-time favourite of legions of shred samurai.

IBANEZ
UNIVERSE

Seven-string guitars are pretty common in rock these days, but back in 1990 when the Universe was launched, it caused quite a stir. The idea of the guitar was the result of a brainstorm between Steve Vai and Ibanez, and he received the first black and green example during the sessions for his seminal 1990 solo album, *Passion And Warfare*.

He not only took to the sonic wonders of the low B-string like a duck to water, but also grabbed an iconic multi-coloured swirl Universe for the sleeve photography, and among a raft of unusual features was the configuration of DiMarzio Blaze II pickups; very few rock guitars at the time came loaded with a central single coil.

The low B is absolutely crushing at rock volumes, with full chords seemingly possessing the sonic ability to level buildings, and Ibanez released an affordable tribute to the original in the Indonesian Premium series in early 2013. As a versatile and eye-catching sevener, the Universe is difficult to beat.

JACKSON

30TH ANNIVERSARY SOLOIST

O kay, you may not be able to fit in your spandex leggings anymore, but if one guitar is going to transport you back to the heady, shreddy days of 1984, it's this. An ultra-limited modern recreation of one of the hair-metal era's most iconic instruments, hand-built by Jackson veteran Mike Shannon, this is as authentic a recreation as you could hope for, down to the size of the control cavity and the spacing of the 'o' and 'n' in the logo. Back in the day, the Soloist appealed to a wider range of users than you'd expect, from the likes of Quiet Riot's Carlos Cavazo to Jeff Beck, and with good reason. This may be an expensive piece of nostalgia, but the 30th Anniversary is just a squirt of hairspray away from perfection.

CHRIS BRODERICK SOLOIST 6

When it came to 80s shred guitars, Jackson was well ahead of the pack with the Soloist. Taking influence from Gibson and Fender with the model's neck construction and body respectively, first examples of the Soloist design predate the official formation of the Jackson Company, back when it was Grover Jackson's side interest during his time at Charvel. Its official debut came in 1984, and models boasted a huge array of finish and pickup custom options, also including Floyd Rose or Kahler trem.

Many different variations on the Soloist have come and gone over the years, and indeed this one is entirely different from those early 'bitsa' creations. In 2012, Jackson's Custom Shop made it for Chris Broderick of metal titans, Megadeth, with a modernized, tweaked and sharpened outline and three-a-side headstock.

JAMES TRUSSART

RUSTY HOLEY STEELCASTER

The offices at *Guitarist* magazine have been blessed over the years with a long and distracting catwalk of guitar temptation. But if there's one single guitar that caused the biggest dent in the team's productivity, it was this work of art. On its arrival, everyone stood around in hushed wonder. That a hollow T-type fashioned from folded steel then buried in the garden should instil such a reaction is a credit to the genius of James Trussart.

It should be as harsh and sharp as razors in lemon juice, but there's a toneful, resonant, compelling surprise in order when you plug this unique guitar in. Equally inviting is the dark-stained maple neck, which is a joy to play. Trussart's range options offer all kinds of permutations, including models incorporating undersaddle transducers and wood, so if you're looking for a truly stunning instrument (and you have the outlay required), a Trussart simply has to be auditioned.

KAUER

DAYLIGHTER JR

Is it a Jazzmaster, a non-reverse Firebird or a Les Paul Junior? Whichever family resemblance you see in this handcrafted, Spanish cedar-bodied looker from Californian maker Doug Kauer, you're bound to be impressed by the heavy blues tones from that Wolfetone P-90.

MALMBERG

MID-90S EXPLORER-STYLE CUSTOM

The guitar you're looking at is something of an oddball that required a fair amount of sleuthing on our part to gather all the details. It was made by a builder called Göran Malmberg, about whom very little is known. However, a guitar of his can be seen in the hands of no less than Eric Clapton in an early Cream video and there are speaker cabinets bearing the Malmberg marque behind Jimmy Page in a Led Zeppelin performance filmed during the late 1960s. Possibly his most celebrated instrument was used by Björn Ulvaeus during ABBA's 1974 Eurovision success in Brighton – remember the guitar shaped like a star? That was made by Göran.

But what about the angular Explorer-type guitar in our picture? It was made for a player called Flavia Canel who played in the Swedish heavy metal band Drain STH. The band flourished for a while, picking up an award or two here and there, including the magazine *Metal Edge*'s 'Female Performers Of The Year' in 1999. Sadly, they disbanded shortly afterwards and Flavia switched to playing bass, which led to this instrument's arrival at Guitars: The Museum in Umeå, Sweden.

From what we can ascertain, the guitar was never meant to be modelled on Gibson's famed Explorer, but instead after a Japanese guitar brand, the exact identity of which seems to have been forgotten by all concerned. Certainly, Ibanez has had some angular body shapes in its catalogue over the years, but the same could be said for a few other Asian makers, too. In any case, it has a carved top and allegedly weighs about the same as two Les Pauls. A brass bridge aids some singing sustain, but many of the guitar's intimate details remain shrouded in mystery. Rare, because there are so few Malmbergs about – all of which adds to the puzzle.

MANSON

MB-1
STANDARD

Matthew Bellamy, frontman for supermassive Devon rockers Muse, has long played various futuristic-looking guitars built to his specs by premier British guitar maker, Hugh Manson at Manson Guitar Works. This limited-edition MB-1, released in 2009, is now one of the Muse man's signature guitars.

Bellamy's ethereal, arena-sized rock style incorporates all kinds of wild, hands-on effects and to this end the MB-1 features an X-Y MIDI control pad that can be used to manipulate other-worldy sounding effects and textures when hooked up to a suitable MIDI sound module.

The elongated T-style chassis also houses a Fernandes Sustainer and a battery to power its gadgetry, but at its heart, it remains a relatively uncomplicated, fit-for-purpose rock guitar to play, albeit one with that's extremely classy and superlatively made, with the finest components. Premium-priced, it's not exactly a purchase to be made on a whim, but then again it's also one of the most expressive electric guitars ever designed: a uniquely imaginative collaboration, just as you'd expect from Bellamy and Manson. The company has also recently expanded its range to include more affordable models.

MARTIN

F-55 1961

Martin's maple-topped F-55, produced between 1961 and 1965, was the company's first single-cut electric model, which borrows elements of its classy aesthetic from Martin's 1930 archtops. This 1961 specimen belongs to US singer-songwriter and vintage-guitar aficionado Jackson Browne, who told us: "It's my new favourite guitar! It has these DeArmond pickups. A lot of Gretsch guitars have these pickups. They sound really great. It's a hollowbody guitar, and very much like the 00-17 in the neck. It's got the same headstock as my other Martins. It's just beautiful: beautiful, in-tune, ringing. It's great for fingerpicking, or anything, really."

PRS

CUSTOM 24
SEMI-HOLLOW

The company's cheaper SE and S2 lines are your first ports of call if you're after a little airflow in your PRS, but this 2014 model is an example of the full USA production line's increasing interest in limited-edition semi-hollowbody designs. Closely following the spec of the current Custom 24 model, with its Pattern Regular neck, uncovered 59/09 pickups and similar body dimensions, the chambered body (hollowed only on the bass side) makes for a lighter weight of 3.1kg (6.82lbs), and adds extra midrange and resonance while retaining the 24's tried-and-trusted character.

PRS

DGT

David Grissom is a Texan guitarist renowned for his supremely tasteful, toneful playing. He was also a prime mover in the development of the 1994 PRS McCarty model; Paul Reed Smith has referred to him as "my ears". After a decade of using McCartys, Grissom was well-placed to move things on to his own signature model.

Outwardly, the DGT appears to be an archetypal PRS, apart from the unusual inclusion of a vibrato unit on a McCarty-spec platform, and a nitrocellulose finish. Like the McCarty, the DGT's body is slightly thicker than a Custom's, while the 22-fret neck features a DGT profile and bigger Dunlop 6100 fretwire. The PAF-style pickups are crucial to the DGT's success: it's like the McCarty has been to the gym and is now more powerful and muscular, yet is still very vintage-like and the coil-splits are most useful and musical. An all-mahogany DGT Standard was released in 2012, too. Whichever you play, look forward to experiencing what we believe could be the ultimate player's PRS.

PRS

S2 SINGLECUT

The original PRS Singlecut caused much legal wrangling with Gibson back in 2000, but still exists in the company's core line in the form of the SC245 and the Mark Tremonti Signature model. This 2014 version is part of the company's recently introduced S2 line, meaning that while it incorporates some Korean-made parts, it's 100 per cent made in Maryland; yet still comes in at roughly half the cost of its swankier sibling. The S2 #7 humbuckers are more midrange-focused than the original Singlecut's versions, and the new S2 leans towards a more contemporary, thrashier voice while remaining vintage-rock focused overall. Favouring build and sound over visual ornamentation, the S2 Singlecut is a reminder that beneath the fancy appointments and the bird inlays, PRS produces superb instruments for the working musician.

RICKENBACKER

ROSE MORRIS (1964) 1997

To the uninitiated, Rickenbacker's model numbering system can be a bit of a maze. The 1997 model was made for Rose Morris who was the European distributor for Rickenbacker in the early 1960s and it was the equivalent of the company's Model 335 – with the 1998, another export model, being the three-pickup version, equivalent to the USA 345. Still with us? Over to Phil Carwardine at Vintage And Modern Guitars... "The 1996 was the Lennon short-scale three-pickup jobby and this is the 1997 two-pickup. The John Lennon baby one; I think they made 21 or 22, so they're really quite rare. Then there's the 1998, which is the [full-size] three-pickup version – Pete Townshend had both, I think, as did Denny Laine who was with The Moody Blues at the time," he tells us.

The 1997's spec comprised a maple semi-hollow body with a double cutaway and a bi-level pickguard. One characteristic that distinguishes the export model from the US version is the f-hole – on American Rickenbackers, this would have been the more familiar curved traditional shape.

According to our sources, only 101 of the 1995 models (based on the US Model 615) were sold, making it quite a rare bird – but there are features that are even less frequently seen. On some models, the position of the f-hole is more 'two o'clock' than the more common 'one o'clock' position. "They go on about the 'two o' clock f-hole'," says Phil. "I think there were around eight made with a two o'clock f-hole. They're incredibly rare."

The 1997 here looks like it has been a resident of the UK for quite a while. "This model has a sticker on the back that says 'Minns Southampton', which is quite nice, thinking that it's been in the UK all this time..." says Phil.

RICKENBACKER
360

This semi-acoustic is very much part of rock 'n' roll heritage; in the hands of George Harrison in the mid-60s, his 1963 prototype Fireglo 12-string 360 (one of only three ever made) would become iconic and not just synonymous with the imagery of The Beatles, but their sound too for the majority of 1964's *A Hard Day's Night*. Roger McGuinn of The Byrds, Tom Petty, Pete Townshend, Peter Buck, Johnny Marr and Paul Weller would also be drawn to the Ricky's unique looks, slimmer neck and chiming tones to follow in the lineage. But some of its features are boldly idiosyncratic; mono and stereo outputs allow for greater creative tonal potential, while the double truss rods were implemented for easier adjustment of the three-ply maple and walnut neck. Just look at it: breathtaking.

SILVERTONE
BOBKAT

In the 1960s in the US, Harmony made guitars for a number of retailers – hence a model ordered from Sears' catalogue would be branded as a Silvertone, and a model branded Airline would be sold by Wards, and so on. Lots were subsequently sold to those budding guitar-mad baby-boomers-on-a-budget, and the resurgence in popularity of these instruments thanks to the muscular-toned retro riffery of Jack White and Dan Auerbach et al has ensured that their price on the vintage market has remained relatively inflated, considering their everyman origins. This diminutive Silvertone Bobkat has DeArmond 'diamond-grille' gold-foil pickups and displays a clear tip of the hat to Fender in its contoured outline. Adrian Utley of Portishead bought this particular one for its "savage" tone.

SILVERTONE

NEWPORT STRATOTONE H42/2 1952

To those not beguiled by vintage student guitars they're a bit of an ugly duckling, but Silvertone guitars have found their way into the hands of many great players, including Muddy Waters, Bob Dylan and one James Marshall Hendrix, who named his 1956 model 'Betty Jean' after his girlfriend at the time.

Silvertone guitars were sold by mail order through Sears, Roebuck & Co, the first electric instruments appearing in the catalogue in the 1940s. The Stratotone was one of the company's popular and affordable models. "There were multiple colours – I think there was a yellow one, a green one and a third one that I can't remember," Phil Carwardine from Vintage And Modern Guitars tells us. "It's a 25 and three-quarter-inch scale length, even though it looks tiny, and so it plays like a full-size guitar. It's got that huge lap-steel neck and it's through construction."

Seeing that the Stratotone was in there during the birth of the revolution in electric guitar manufacture at the beginning of the 1950s, it's surprising to note that the electronic design here is really ahead of its time. "With this amazing single-coil pickup, it sounds like a really big-bodied archtop," Phil continues. "Wiring is on a dual-concentric pot – volume and tone – and I don't know how they thought of it, but they've got that switch that takes the tone out of the circuit, which is quite a thought-through thing. So you get the full blast of the pickup out."

And what about that Hendrix connection? "Jimi's first guitar was this model, but it changed shape and so his was slightly different, but it was a Stratotone..."

TOM ANDERSON
RAVEN

T he Raven is one of the least ornamented and 'posh' Andersons. This subtly downsized take on a surfy familiar is actually the Californian maker's favourite among his instruments, and when you play one, you'll appreciate why. Although Fender's Jazzmaster is the clear aesthetic inspiration here, beyond retaining the large scratchplate, this is a very different instrument. It's lightweight, has a choice of scale lengths, and while those pickups may look like the Jazzmaster's original P-90 units, they're actually tiltable mini-humbuckers which sound like slightly cleaned-up P-90s. They're tougher than single-coils, but not as sophisticated as full-size 'buckers, and as result, the Raven actually leads the player in a more alt-rock direction than you'd expect from an upmarket instrument. An Anderson with attitude? You bet.

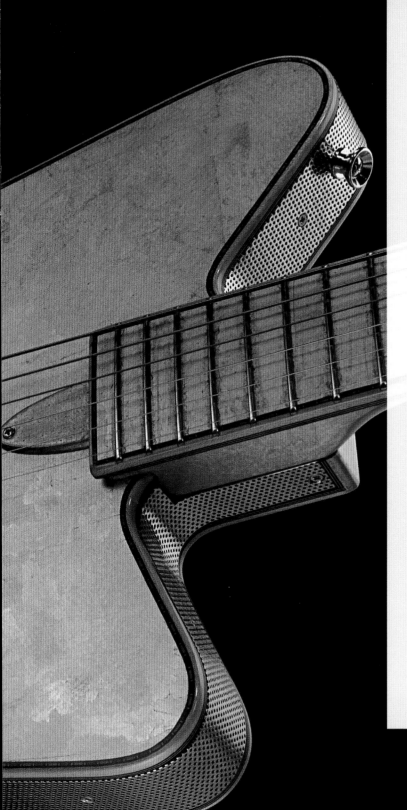

RAYA BILLY F GIBBONS BLUE LIGHT SPECIAL

In 2006, while flying back to Finland from the NAMM show in Anaheim, Helsinki luthier Kari Nieminen of Versoul Instruments was flicking through Billy F Gibbons' *Rock + Roll Gearhead* book and wondering what kind of guitar he'd design for the ZZ Top man, one of his favourite players. The Atlantic Ocean played its part in fixing the idea of blue light in Kari's mind, and upon his return, he crafted the instrument that became the Raya Billy F Gibbons Blue Light Special.

Based on his Raya model, the twin blue cast-glass lenses on each side of the body have LEDS which light up when the guitar is plugged in. The industrial theme is extended by perforated chrome-plated steel sides and the electric razor style pickup cover, while the 23-carat gold leaf finish on the alder body and headstock tempers the design with a more organic, autumnal quality.

Gibbons ordered a further five more variations, with chambered bodies, extra inlays, necks covered in gold leaf, a Baritone setup, a vibrato and a black finish.

WASHBURN

PARALLAXE PXS20FRTBB

Washburn's 2013 Parallaxe electrics are a deliberate reminder of the company's place in history as a foundry for innovative metal instruments. Metal players and shredders alike will be licking their lips at the sight of the PXS20's pointy headstock, Stephen's Extended Cutaway, Buzz Feiten tuning system and, of course, that double-locking Floyd Rose, which comes fitted with rubber dampeners on the springs to cure the notorious Floyd rattle. A mahogany body, loaded with Seymour Duncan TB-6B and SH-1 Jazz pickups, ensures a rounded, meaty rock rhythm tone; when it comes to solo time, the gloss-finished neck with its 24-jumbo-fret baked-ebony 'board makes shredding up at the dusty end an addictive pleasure. A genuinely impressive modern guitar that sees Washburn return to its roots with gusto.

YAMAHA

PACIFICA 112

T he Pacifica, originally designed by Yamaha's Hollywood-
based Custom Shop, is the brand's best-selling electric guitar
by a mile or two: the company counts well over a million units
shifted. Solid alder bodies, as opposed to laminate, afforded the
Pacifica unique status in the entry-level market when the budget
012 and 112 models launched in 1993.

Yamaha is known for its quality and consistency. Originally, the
Pacifica was made in Yamaha's Taiwanese factory, before moving
to the company's facility in Indonesia a couple of years back. Did
anyone notice any difference? No. They were probably too busy
comparing the specs of what is now a greatly expanded range,
with some higher-end models recently added.

Decent quality hardware, good pickups (upgraded in 2007) and
a proper fret job and set-up make this the ideal starter student
guitar or a more-than-reliable backup. It's perfect for upgrading,
too. Every home should have one!

YAMAHA
SG2000VW

The original SG2000 was a trailblazer in 1976 – a professional-level Japanese-made guitar that found its way into the hands of a diverse range of players from Bob Marley to Steve Cropper. But the first and most influential was Carlos Santana, whose feedback on the company's first designs for the guitar would lead to a thicker body for added resonance, and a brass plate connected to the tailpiece for sustain. This vintage white version pictured was launched in 2009, and limited to a run of just 50 guitars, but retains the model's early key features: 'T Cross' neck-through-body construction (two pieces of mahogany surrounding the main maple part); the coil-tapped humbuckers that had been implemented in 1979; and the brass Sustain Plate. Initial Response Acceleration brings a touch of modern technology to this model; Yamaha's solution of relieving the stresses between the guitar's materials in the construction process to save the time and effort it takes for a guitarist to 'play in' a guitar.